MY WORLD

MY WORLD

The Extraordinary Life of Gail Taylor

AN AUTOBIOGRAPHY

Foreword by Sir Harry Secombe

The Book Guild Ltd
Sussex, England

The Book Guild Ltd.
25 High Street,
Lewes, Sussex

First published 1997
© Gail Taylor, 1997
Reprinted 1998

Set in Times

Typesetting by
Raven Typesetters, Chester

Printed in Great Britain by
Bookcraft (Bath) Ltd, Avon

A catalogue record for this book is
available from the British Library

ISBN 1 85776 210 X

FOR GAIL

I first had the pleasure of meeting Gail some years ago in an hotel close to my home. Her mother informed me that we had a mutual friend in Sir Geraint Evans. I was very impressed by the way she handled her disability and the happiness which exuded from her.

I will not pre-empt the story she has to tell but I will say that it is a tale of great courage and determination in which she writes of her frustration at being unable to communicate with others, of the breakthrough to the outside world, and of the devotion of her parents.

She teaches us to set aside the outward signs of disability and to look instead at the real person inside.

Inside Gail there is a truly remarkable person who has mastered six languages – French, Italian, Spanish, Portuguese, German and Russian; has a great knowledge of music and the IQ of a small township.

This is a beautiful book by a beautiful soul and I recommend it to everyone.

(Sir Harry Secombe)

v

PREFACE BY MY MOTHER

Ken and I married on 5 April 1951. Gail was born prematurely on 31 October 1951, weighing just under 2 pounds. Such an early birth (she was due on 28 January the following year) was, in those days, considered a miscarriage. We had very little money, no car, no home of our own, and a honeymoon baby born prematurely.

I was certainly not prepared for such an event. Before my marriage my Mother had spoilt me. I had my own car, money was something I did not have to worry about, and I socialised extensively. Now this! Gail had to spend the first three months of her life in hospital, and during this time she appeared to respond to no outside influence whatsoever. No one told us that she was in any way disabled. We both assumed she was possibly backward because she was premature.

We were eventually allowed to take her home, but my feelings towards her were anything but maternal. Unless Gail was continually being nursed, she screamed. Every visitor, or knock on the door, or unusual noise, just worsened the situation, her screams becoming louder and more insistent.

Looking after Gail was extremely stressful. If it had not been for Ken, and my Mother, who were both wonderfully patient with her, I could easily have put her into a home.

We could never go out, and we could never have friends or relatives to visit, as Gail created total disruption with her crying and screaming. Ken and my Mother were convinced that given continual care and loving, we would get through this agonising period. But I looked after her the majority of the time, and I was not convinced by their argument – this little monster was driving me to distraction.

Poor Gail, she must have been so insecure, so bewildered, so unhappy. The medical profession were loath to tell us of the extent of her disabilities. It was not until Gail was a year old that an eye specialist, without preamble, told us that Gail was totally blind. (Apparently, during the early days when Gail required oxygen this treatment had had a severe effect, and had blinded her.) Gail was six years old before the council medical officer advised that Gail had cerebral palsy, and that with all her other disabilities, she would never walk.

To imagine what Gail had to endure, try shutting your eyes for one hour, without talking and not moving your body. This is what Gail went through for the first nine years of her life.

It is with regret that I admit that I did not attempt to teach Gail anything. I did not think it was worth trying, let alone perservering. How wrong could I have been? I did, however, read to her a great deal, seeing that it appeared to please her, but I assumed it was because I held her and gave her my full attention. I now know that I was mistaken. Gail was trying to find a way to communicate.

As Gail will tell you later I used to read a *Brer Rabbit* book to her, over and over again, and one day, miraculously, Gail's little hand stretched out and turned the page when I had reached the end. She was six years old, could not sit up unaided, could not see or speak, but she had broken through these barriers, which told me that she had a functioning mind. There was no stopping us. Now I really had something to work on. And so it started.

None of her subsequent achievements would have been possible without the unfailing love and support Ken has given both Gail and me throughout our lives together. Without him, Gail could not have become the person she is today, and I would not have known the joy of having such a daughter as I have. I have learnt so much from Gail.

Gail's condition, in a strange way, has not been a handicap. She cannot see her own disabilities which to able-bodied people are visually severe, and at times unnerving. She has taught me so much more than I have taught her. Her patience and love are overwhelming. Her superb brain and her thirst for learning are amazing. Gail sees no need for criticism of anybody, or anything. She never fails to thank us for what we do for her during the day. She never fails to thank me after each meal, nor for giving her a bath. She never fails to thank me and her Father for a lovely day when we kiss goodnight. Gail's charm, her love, which she gives freely, and the happiness which she radiates, make up for all the work, the worries, the anxieties, the fears. Ken and I feel so humble. What more can we say about our darling daughter? It has been, and continues to be, a rewarding life, and a privilege to look after her and to share with her the wonder of her world.

Our love, admiration and respect for Gail grows daily.

God has indeed blessed Gail, and us.

Pam Taylor

1

Born the first and only child (my parents believing in quality rather than quantity), three months premature and weighing just under two pounds, the first three months of my life were spent in an incubator, my having great difficulty in breathing. The hospital had administered too much oxygen which unfortunately deprived me of my sight. A condition known as retrolental fibroplasia. My parents were not told of my condition until I was a year old. Consequently I was treated as a normal baby. My mother often put me outside in the pram, leaving me to sleep.

I also suffered from epilepsy, having frequent fits. I have never been able to walk, and therefore have to stay in a wheelchair. I have limited movement in my hands and arms. As you will read I could not speak until I was nine years old. Life was very tough for me in the beginning, with these disabilities, and all the doctors and specialists said I would be a 'cabbage' all my life and that my parents should not waste time looking after me. But I persevered, and with the help and guidance of my parents every inch of the way, and marvellous friends and tutors, and teaching myself through radio and television, I have created a life.

I consider myself to be a very lucky person to live the

way I do, surrounded by love. You see, what I cannot do doesn't worry me. I have so many things to learn about and so many friends. Forget about the disabilities and the body I am in. Look at the person inside, and you will find that, basically, I am no different from you. I do not experience as much of life as you do, as I lead a very protected life. This has its advantages and disadvantages – my emotions are not as mature as they should be, but maybe this is an advantage, because as you get older you become more wary and cynical in general. Whereas in my world everyone is loving, kind, helpful and affectionate. I see nothing of the cruelties and unpleasantness as everyone treats me as a special person, and they are always willing to help me in any way they can.

I hope this book will help you to understand the problems of people like myself. If you meet a severely disabled person along the way, I hope reading this will help you to cope and accept them as you would anyone else. Just remember that their achievement of picking up a cup and taking it to their lips could be like you running a four-minute mile.

I hope this book may help other disabled people, particularly those suffering from cerebral palsy and who cannot speak, and the people who are looking after them. Often a disabled person's body can be badly misshapen but their minds are usually intact. If you are able to give them a little of your time and show patience, you may be able to release them from their isolation, and make them more acceptable to society. For example, all my tutors say teaching me has been very rewarding, and has given them great satisfaction.

I think that more than most people I can appreciate the trauma and frustration felt by both John McCarthy and Terry Waite. That part of my life when I was unable to communicate is definitely a closed chapter which I can never speak about. Please remember there are hundreds of people like me in the world – give them your help, time and understanding if you are able. They all want to be part of society, not just to be loved, fed and kept clean as you would a pet. Make them as lucky as I have been – you will find it very rewarding.

I expect you are wondering how someone with my disabilities can 'write' a book, and I must confess, it is with great difficulty. So again I turn to good friends to help me. I have dictated most of the book on tape, or with my mother or Father writing it down in longhand.

I would like to thank Annette Shaw, who is a journalist, for typing up my recordings and helping us with a rough draft manuscript which was sent to the publishers, to see if my story would be acceptable to them. They seemed very pleased with what I had 'written', so for the last six months my story has been completed and updated.

Without help, this would not have been possible. My special appreciation goes to friends of long standing – Shirley and Tony Ewen. Tony has given up a lot of his time to reconstruct and bring my autobiography up to the present time. Without his help it would have been almost impossible to complete. I first met Tony, and later Shirley, his wife, when Tony entertained clients at the hotel, and booked in many overseas clients. When coming to the hotel he would first make a point of having a short chat with me – and from there our friendship blossomed. Tony introduced me to Shirley, who also loves music, so no wonder we get on so well. We all meet regularly and enjoy each other's company.

Gail – a very special person

It was about 16 years ago when we first saw Gail in the Bramley Grange Hotel, owned at that time by her parents. It was obvious that Gail was severely disabled, but we disputed with each other as to whether she was totally blind. We had heard her say to friends 'How lovely to see you again'. 'Did you see the snooker last night?' 'I saw the golf yesterday, wasn't it exciting?' It was difficult to believe that she could not see.

Subsequently, having become friends of the family, we knew that Gail could see nothing as understood by a sighted person, but had her own particular gift of 'sight'. As we began to know her better, we soon realised that Gail was determined that her disabilities would not prevent her from living her life to the fullest extent. Many able-bodied people lack the stamina and perseverance to learn or acquire the astonishing range of talents possessed by Gail. How many people have perfect musical pitch? How many people can speak seven languages? How many people have totally retentive memories with an encyclopedic knowledge of all types of music? How many people can qualify as Radio Amateurs?

Now Gail has told her remarkable story. But the story is not over. We are certain that Gail will continue to confound the doubts of many. She proves, every day, that disablement does not prevent achievement and happiness in life. She continues her fight with a dismissive attitude towards her disabilities, and with a fine sense of humour. Above all she has an enviable awareness of how good life can be.

As Gail says, 'You may be interested to know ...

We are interested, Gail, we really are.

What's next?

Shirley and Tony Ewen

4

2

I think it would be nice, and in fact essential to the story, if you also got to know my parents. After all, none of this would have happened without them! Obviously it isn't possible for me to tell how it all began, but with help from my parents, I think I can give you a good account of the family background, as my parents and I have talked a lot about it over the years.

It has to be said that my Mother and Father build their whole life around me. I know that all parents do this to an extent, but with me, there is no apparent end in sight! They could have abandoned me at birth and put me in a home. They are two people very much in love with life and each other. They could have been bitter and resentful, but to what end? In an odd sort of way, I've enriched their lives, and I know that I've taught them tolerance and patience. For example, one of them will come and start to wheel me into the dining room for lunch, then the phone goes. Ten minutes later I am still waiting, but what choice do I have? My Father openly admits that at one time his priority would have been the next cricket match, but when you start to consider life from where I sit, your priorities change.

Curiously, the lives of my parents, Pamela and Kenneth Taylor, ran parallel long before they married. It really is a lovely story, the girl-meets-boy-next-door routine, and Mother often jokes that she was virtually molested in her pram! They were even born in the same maternity home, Kenneth Walter Taylor on 13 May 1921 and Pamela Doreen Gill on 16 April 1924. They lived on opposite sides of the same road in Catford, which in those days was a smart London suburb in SE6. Although not exactly silver-spoon territory, both families had a maid and Father began prep school with my Mother's elder sister.

Then the Gill family moved to Rose Walk, a private estate in Purley, in 1929, as my maternal Grandfather worked for the County of London Electricity Company, where he was secretary to the chairman. At this point the contact was lost, as the Taylors went to live in Beckenham. Both were bright and well-educated and very keen on sport, Mother at Croydon High School and Father at St Dunstan's College, Catford.

They tell me they didn't meet at all during the war years, although they did hear about each other whilst serving in the forces. In 1939 Father joined the Royal Air Force, along with his brother, my uncle Alan, who became a navigator at Bomber Command and was ultimately awarded the DFC. Sadly he was killed in action towards the end of the war. He had volunteered for a sortie when he was supposed to have been on a rest period, having flown 30 missions. The night he died, my Father remembers lying in bed, and suddenly looking at the clock. It was 11.55 p.m. He was about to turn off the light, when he saw a round dish with a bright glow just above the curtain. He put the light off and on again but the disc had gone. The following day the incident was still very much on his mind, and he mentioned it to a friend in London, adding the comment he was glad Alan was on rest, because the RAF had lost a lot of bombers the previous night. When he got home there was a telegram. Alan had been shot down

6

at 11.55 p.m. It may interest you to know that, strangely, a similar thing happened to Mother when Nana died. I mention these incidents because my parents firmly believe that the departing souls of Alan and Nana were saying good-bye. The sister at the nursing home, confirmed that she had similar experiences, whilst on duty and agreed she thought it was the soul departing.

Father's own flying career didn't last throughout the war. He was posted to Brighton, initially, to begin the pilot training course. While the powers that be were organising training, he was sent to patrol the seafront, along with other new recruits. Their weapons for use against the Third Reich were broomsticks with bayonets attached. Fortunately, there was no invasion. Having begun formal flight training, my Father reckons his eyesight let him down and claims to have been a potential hazard to the RAF. Since they were keen to keep aircraft losses attributable only to the German Luftwaffe, he was discharged after 15 months and, was obliged to work on the land as a farm labourer to help the war effort.

Mother joined the Wrens and at one time was the only Wren attached to a base consisting of 46 sailors at Gashouse Creek, Harwich. She also served in Scotland. She was a coder Wren, although she admits to never actually coding or decoding a message. The work usually involved secretarial duties for the base commander, and illicit trips around the coast in motor torpedo boats.

Now that the war is well and truly past, I am going to tell the truth. Apparently my Mother used to go to sea and sit up in the MTB boats cockpit, watching all the destroyers lined up at anchor. If the other crews saw a Wren on board, they would hoist the gin pennant. A signal would come to take the officers and Wren on board – for drinks!

Immediately after the war, my Mother and Father went back to normal life, working and playing hard. My Father reluctantly took over a failing family business, which at the time was supporting his two uncles and my Grandmother.

My Mother worked in an estate agents as secretary to a director. Then her Father started a building business, and made her a partner, so she was kept very busy. Both my parents continued to play a great deal of sport, my Father playing cricket, rugby and squash, and my Mother playing tennis and squash. They used to meet at the Old Dunstonians school sports club (which had been founded by my Grandfather).

By 1950 they were courting seriously, and got engaged. Father wanted to wait five years until he had some money, but Mother said 'No way', because that would have made her age 30, so they compromised and got married six months later. The wedding took place in 1951 at Beckenham, Kent, although from what they tell me it's a wonder they made it down the aisle.

My Mother and Father used to go off to cricket matches, and it was whilst returning from a game played near Sevenoaks, that my Father, who was driving my Mother's Triumph roadster, hit a bus coming towards them head on.

They were taken to Farnborough Hospital, where they found that my Mother had broken two front teeth and needed a number of stitches to her mouth. This did not bode well for my Mother's modelling career, certainly until she got her teeth fixed, which I understand took quite a few months.

When my Father took my Mother home the next day to her parents, her Father immediately piled into my Mother, saying, 'I warned you of this tearing around the country-side at high speed.'

'I am sorry, sir,' said my Father, 'but I was driving.'

'Ah!' said my Grandfather. 'Well, these things happen, don't they?'

It is worth mentioning that when my Mother and Father got engaged to be married, my Grandfather asked my Father if he was really serious. When he replied yes, my Grandfather said, 'You want your (bleep) brains tested! She will have you in the bankruptcy court in six months.' How wrong he was. Still, I think my Grandfather was really very fond of my Mother and probably it was said tongue in cheek.

Another time, in Cambridge, after a cricket match my Father punted his fiancee serenely and romantically down the river Cam, hit a bridge, and Mother hurtled headlong into the murky waters. She travelled home dressed in cricket gear, borrowed from my Father.

After honeymooning in Devon, they house-hunted, without success. Eventually the servants' quarters (bedrooms, garages and stables) of a big old house in Beckenham were converted by my Grandfather's company into a delightful L-shaped cottage. They had to work hard on the house and received no help from their families. In fact Grandfather charged them £1,500 more than the original quote, so they had to sell their car to pay him. The house was subsequently sold to the late Sir (then Mr) Geraint Evans, who became a close family friend and my Godfather.

In the midst of all this, my Father continued to run the family business. This was the manufacture of children's coats, but it could afford neither a good cutter nor a good designer, and consequently all the work was carried out by long-serving, elderly employees. My Father was forced into the role of salesman, as well as his other duties. He loathed having to do this, and was, understandably, not particularly successful. One evening in the bar of his sports club, he met the receptionist of a famous London modelling agency who said that they were looking for a male model, 6 feet tall, with a 44-inch chest, and more importantly, photogenic. Would he be interested? Remembering that a few years previously he had been offered a film test (which he had refused as 'not his cup of tea') he decided to investigate further. As a result he did a great deal of photographic modelling work, for Ford cars and sweaters, working with the actor Roger Moore, known later as The Saint, before his most famous role as James Bond. It may also interest you to know, that my Father was the first man to model the new C & A mens range.

Mother found she was pregnant eight weeks after they were married. There was no reason for concern and everything to look forward to. There were no difficulties during the pregnancy, and she remembers being pleased that she still looked very slim. Then suddenly, late one night, she got very bad pains and the labour started. An ambulance was called and, somewhat alarmingly, neither the hospital nor maternity home would accept responsibility, on the grounds they did not take miscarriages and weren't about to start! Mother carried me for only 26 weeks and no one really believed a baby of this term would survive. At that time, the early 1950s, premature baby units simply did not exist as they do today.

Eventually, the family doctor persuaded the maternity home to accept her as a patient. Incidentally, the comedian Bob Monkhouse's son Gary was born there, just the day before, with a birth weight of under 2 pounds. As you will read, our families kept in touch for some time.

My Father remembers the next 12 hours as being very anxious, full of concern for Mother and how she was feeling. He says he stayed at home, silently staring at the wall, because this was a long time before the days when Fathers were encouraged to be in a delivery room and present at the birth. The weather that day, 31 October 1951, was horrendous – wild and windy. At 5 p.m. I was born.

10

Weighing only 1 pound 13 ounces, I was a tiny scrap of a thing, described by Mother as the proverbial 'ugly duckling', and by Father as a baby bird which had fallen out of a nest. The hospital put me in an incubator and suggested, with as much tact as possible, a quick baptism – because the medical staff thought it was unlikely I would be alive in the morning. Because of the storm, the name which my parents felt was the most appropriate was Gale. So I was christened there and then: Gale Anne Taylor, later changed to Gail.

3

As I am sure you can imagine, my chances of survival were extremely slim. My birth weight dropped, and from what I have heard, I just lay motionless in my incubator. My Mother was the only person on the ward not able to feed her new baby and she was left, in a very fragile state, to cope with her emotions. The birth had not been easy for her, because I was also a breach delivery. Apparently the labour was long and Mother says the staff were not very pleased with her because she had not been to the exercise and pre-natal classes, but as she pointed out, she was not due to even begin them until the following week. She remembers that I emerged feet first and then a senior consultant just got hold of me and pulled me out. It was a horrendous shock for both of us. Mother says it felt as though her whole body was being wrenched away.

Have you ever seen a picture of a premature baby? I am told they look revolting, covered in a sort of white or grey down. There is no flesh, just skin, almost transparent, showing the veins underneath. I didn't cry. I squeaked. While still in the delivery room, Mother asked my Father to tell her what I looked like. It must have been awful for him to have to explain.

My Mother is open and honest. She had no real feelings of my belonging to her, no sense of bonding with me at all.

Her maternal instincts were just not there at this time, compounded by the fact the other Mothers in the ward used to express milk for me. Artificial food didn't seem to suit me and I went from being a dark colour to jaundiced yellow. In the next incubator lay little Gary Monkhouse, some 6 ounces less than I weighed and also severely disabled with cerebral palsy. My Father visited every day and he says that Mother was usually crying. She used to knit to pass the time and the staff gave her an apple to gauge the size of my head. But she was quite depressed and I believe visiting times were far from happy.

Every morning, my Father rang the hospital, to be told that I was alive but not to build up any hopes. Mother returned home after ten days, so at least they were facing things together. Still they rang the hospital every morning, only to be told there was little change. They came each day to the hospital and looked at me in my little life-supporting glass incubator.

My parents had only been married six months and so my Grandfather came to the hospital once, just to make sure I was a premature baby. He never discussed me again, seeming shocked. My Father was afraid to register the birth, as he felt it might bring bad luck – and I wouldn't survive. In those days you were allowed six weeks to register a birth so after a month, they went to see the Registrar.

But I survived and three months passed. So came the day when I was brought home, with instructions that I was to be fed every two hours, including all through the night. The renovations on the cottage were not complete and although my Grandfather was wealthy, he did not offer any help. There was no choice but to live with one or other of our in-laws, which did not make for a very happy situation, but at least I was home, and we were a family. I think Mother was quite proud of me, although any deep mater-

13

nal feelings were still a bit vague. She acknowledges she could easily have been persuaded to put me in a home – my Father, jokingly, always said he would file for a divorce if she even gave it another thought, or if there was any bitterness. Nana was Mother's main source of emotional support and she was wonderful with me. They were all anxious regarding the progress I might or might not make and what the future would hold. It was Nana who said that they should remember I was a real person trapped inside this body and they were the only ones who could help me. Fortunately for me and against all advice, from family, friends and our doctor, they decided to persevere. The GP even said my brain had been so severely damaged during birth, that there was no hope, no point in building their lives around me. As my Father has always maintained, no one should be told there is no hope. Someone, somewhere may be on the verge of discovering a cure for any illness or disability. You should never give up. There is always hope.

As I grew, it was Nana who gave me a lot of love, took me out and gave Mother a much-needed break from round-the-clock caring. If anyone called or even rang the doorbell, I would scream and scream and then scream some more. Mother began to wonder if there was any intelligence at all, any capability of thinking, in my head. But life went on and when we went out she always took me in the shops with her, carrying me on her hip. I was fine in food shops, but if we went into a chemist's, all hell would break loose. But this told Mother something – that I could differentiate between smells. Chemists reminded me of hospitals, but food shops were all right. Some of the shopkeepers used to chat to me, even though they never got a response, and the greengrocer was particularly nice. It got so that I would actually sit by the till whilst they served Mother. But this caused a queue and we were not very popular in town.

It was very hard for my family. Socially they did nothing. They couldn't go out and couldn't have visitors because I was such a screaming monster. The only thing that kept me happy was if either Mother or Nana held me, fed me or sang to me. Perhaps it was then, that my love for music started. In the words of the pop group Abba, I say, 'Thank you for the music.'

When my Father came home in the evening, he tried to help by sitting me on his lap and talking to me, but I just screamed. Life was more than tough and nobody got much sleep. One night he rocked me in my cot hour after hour. Every time he stopped, I screamed. When we talked about this for the book, he said that come the morning, he could cheerfully have thrown me out of the window.

As time progressed, providing chemist shops and other people's homes were avoided, I settled down. Then, just to put another spoke in the wheel, I became epileptic. Distressing for everyone else to see, let alone for me! The family doctor said they should put me in a home, forget me, and start again. But with parents like mine, there was no chance of that. They thought I was making progress, albeit slowly. But another blow was waiting around the corner. Our doctor thought I had a weak heart. Then soon after that there was concern over my sight.

My parents had thought everything was all right and admitted that when you have a baby, you want everything to be perfect. I didn't sit up or do anything, but since I was premature, everyone assumed I was a late developer. Even the health visitor failed to spot anything drastic. When I was ten months old, because my eyes did not appear to focus, the doctor sent us to an eye specialist in London. He put drops in my eyes and said very bluntly, that I was blind. Although I have no memory of any of this, I am sure that even as a baby, it must have registered somewhere. All these people telling Mother and Father that I was useless, a complete write-off, blind, epileptic, spastic, a cabbage. All of this was said in front of me on the basis that I couldn't understand, but I did. I took it in. Mother thinks that a lot of harm was caused and that my confidence must have taken blow after blow, until it was practically destroyed.

The shock of finding I was blind was overwhelming for them, and all my Father remembers is that in the next breath the specialist asked him to settle the account. Ignoring the financial aspect for a moment, my parents, still stunned, repeated the diagnosis. What do you mean blind? Completely blind? Can anything be done? Can we give an eye each? No, said the specialist, nothing can be done, and asked again to have his account settled. My Father told him to send the account. It may interest you to know that, over 40 years later, emotions still run high in our family and we would all like a chance to tell the specialist to show some compassion when giving patients such bad news.

We drove home in a borrowed car, stunned. What transpired, as Mother and Father pieced together the story, was that pure oxygen given to me after the birth, while to all intents and purposes I was still developing in the incubator, had caused a condition known as retrolental fibroplasia. This means that a permanent, inoperable shield grew over the back of the retina of each of my eyes. I was never going to see.

My Father made up his mind that he would never play cricket or squash again, never watch the television; in other words, never do anything that a blind person couldn't do. He was that shocked.

He borrowed the car again the next day to take Mother to a hotel for lunch. My Father looked at the beautiful gardens of the hotel and thought, 'Gail will never see this.' They sat in the restaurant, unable to eat anything.

16

4

For most people the first birthday is celebrated and remembered. Not so for us. The epilepsy which I mentioned earlier continued for the next nine years. Although each fit only lasted a minute or so, it was extremely frightening for everyone. Mother had to put a toothbrush between my teeth to stop me biting my tongue and just hold me until the convulsions stopped. Our doctor suggested a tranquillising drug to keep me calm and to give them some peace and quiet, but my parents decided against this and said they would rather try to cope, being quite against drugs unless absolutely essential. They were also concerned that if I were to be subdued all the time, what chance would I have of ever developing?

One night they put me in the bathroom so that they could have some sleep, but about 2 a.m. I had a fit. They heard an awful gurgling and had to dash in and pick me up. On another occasion when visitors called, I was upstairs in a carrycot screaming. A bit of cotton I'd pulled from the blanket was cutting my fingers. The more I struggled the worse it got.

Really, I needed full-time one-to-one care. I suffered from bronchitis a lot, and my parents got virtually no sleep. Father remembers another night, when I had been sick several times. At about 3.30 a.m. they brought a tray of tea back to bed. Mother put the tray on the floor, but I was about to be sick again, so she rushed over to the cot, my Father following to help. He stepped into the middle of the tray, and everything went flying. They sat on the edge of the bed, in silence. My Father, ever optimistic, decided that one day we were all going to laugh about it. The tension broke. We really believe a sense of humour saved many a situation when everyone could so easily have cracked.

The early years seemed to merge into each other and Mother says, in all honesty, that the first two or three years were like living a nightmare. They were still suffering from terrible shock. Every specialist they took me to really gave no hope of my ever developing my mind at all, and my physical state was very poor. We never went out and hardly had any visitors. One exception was Elizabeth Monkhouse, with her baby Gary, who was able to travel easily because she had a car. Husband Bob was away a lot, although he popped in after some shows. My Father remembers that it was comforting to have someone in similar circumstances to chat about things. They supported each other, but as with many of life's tougher experiences, it is hard and painful to recall. Bob Monkhouse wrote a lovely letter not long ago, sending his best wishes for the success of this book.

Introducing me to new foods was difficult, and so was weaning on to solid foods. At the age of five I still had a bottle and was not toilet trained; that took a lot of patience. Mother sat me on the potty and poured cold water between my thighs, to try to make me understand I was supposed to be doing it myself. It took six months before the penny dropped. She grunted, to get across the idea of a bowel movement, and until I learned to talk that was the only way I could indicate my need to go to the loo.

Nana was a tower of strength, and she took us away on

holiday, to a bungalow in Pevensey Bay. Rather than being a much-needed rest, it was a disaster! The house reeked of dry rot; I'm afraid I took an instant dislike to it and screamed for two days. In desperation we all came home.

And then when I was four and a half, I was finally diagnosed as being spastic. Whilst most babies crawled and tried to walk, I stayed put. As a premature baby, and bearing in mind the blindness, it had been accepted that my physical development was slower than normally expected. I could walk on tiptoe, with Mother and Father either side, supporting me. The health visitor asked a doctor from Social Services to call and he left us in no doubt as to the future. There was not going to be much of one. With no apparent consideration for anyone's feelings or with any compassion, he pointed out, that I had cerebral palsy and that's why I wasn't walking. It was so matter-of-fact. He was probably under the impression that my parents were already aware of my spastic condition.

Once again my parents were both in a state of shock and at first the news didn't penetrate. Then it slowly dawned and they began to ask questions. What is cerebral palsy? They looked up the meaning in the dictionary. To some doctors it is probably all in a day's work. An explanation or just a little time to talk things through would have made a world of difference; I must have felt the atmosphere. I may be blind, but my senses are more finely tuned than most people's. Mother and Father had no doubts about where they stood, but were a long way from accepting anything without a fight.

I visited a physiotherapist, who was in charge of the Cerebral Palsy Unit in Lambeth Hospital, and who was also involved in a day centre at Carshalton Hospital. Unfortunately, she was, in my opinion, an exceptionally cold and unfeeling person, totally lacking compassion or understanding. It was obvious she had taken an instant dislike to the three of us. She considered me very spoilt, but she had the opinion that if she was granted total control over me, she would be able to teach me to walk and talk.

Our consultation with her was a complete nightmare for me. I considered then, and I still do now, that she was unforgivingly callous. She stripped me of my clothes, hung me upside down, and blew a whistle in my ear. My Mother came near to hitting her, but restrained herself, as she had been highly recommended, and the hope was there that she could help me. I just screamed and screamed. What was this awful woman doing – and more fearfully, what was she going to do next?

She suggested that I attended her day clinic, and despite my parents' misgivings (you must remember that they were willing to explore every avenue to improve my quality of life), we went to it.

Without any words of explanation, and treating me as a 'thing' rather than as a person, she took me and sat me at a wooden table in an armless chair specially made for a person of my size so that my feet touched the ground. Whilst this may have been reassuring for some, to me it felt very strange, and I started shaking, and hanging onto the table.

She told (ordered?) my Mother to leave. Unbeknown to me, my Mother stood outside, watching through a window. Apparently I cried and screamed for two hours, and the staff were forbidden to go near me until I had quietened down. My Mother, as you may imagine, was becoming more and more distressed. It is difficult to believe that this type of 'treatment' could be allowed to happen.

Lunch was brought round by the staff, and the food was put in front of me. Still they had instructions not to speak to me. Whimpering, I fell asleep with my face in the food. This was too much for my Mother. She went to see the sister in charge and asked her advice. The sister said that she could not take responsibility for me, and my Mother decided that 'enough was enough' – gathered me up, put me in the car, and took me to my Grandmother.

Nana was horrified when told of what had happened. Whilst my Mother was so upset, my Grandmother cuddled and comforted me, and put me to bed. It became apparent that I was running a temperature, and the doctor was called out. He diagnosed bronchitis, which turned to pneumonia. I was ill for about three weeks, and it took me a year to regain my confidence.

My Father was so angry that he arranged a meeting with the lady concerned, together with the head of the hospital, and told them exactly what he thought about the physiotherapist and her treatment of me. He would prefer that I made no progress, and remained happy, rather than be subjected to such mental cruelty. So this unhappy episode ended. We never saw her again. Neither did we wish to.

5

After that, as far as possible we established our own routine. My Father went back to playing cricket and rugby. Mother enjoyed the occasional game of squash. She read to me for hours at a time, and, it may interest you to know, she allowed me to tear up greaseproof paper because I liked the sound of it, and it was the one thing I could do.

Apart from that, the only thing that interested me was close physical contact with either Mother or Nana. It was during a reading session that Mother realised that I knew when it was time to turn the page. I was desperate to get through somehow, and it occurred to me that if I reached out and turned a page, Mother would perhaps realise that I understood something.

It worked! My first breakthrough! It was also my first chance to show what a phenomenal memory I have, because I knew when the last words on each page were coming up.

Mother set out to prove I had an intellect, and bought a pegboard with shapes on it. Over about a year I learned to feel and identify the wooden pieces, four each of triangles, squares, circles and oblongs. Things were looking up. When I could successfully fit the shapes on the board, Mother then taught me to count.

We all turned our attention to family life, and started

socialising a little. My Father bought a Ford Popular car, so Mother was able to drive over to Nana's at Purley. The next aim was for us to have a purpose-built house to accommodate my special needs, so my Father bought a plot of land at Park Langley near Beckenham, and built a chalet bungalow, with two bedrooms downstairs. Upstairs there was a self-contained flat. The hope was that we could find a couple to live there rent-free in return for baby-sitting.

After a few disastrous choices, a newly married couple called Betty and Leonard Norris moved in. Betty was an infant school teacher, and Leonard, or Uncle Mud as I knew him, was a Customs officer. They were both very caring and were prepared to spend time getting to know me and we became very fond of each other. They even took me to their parents' home in Broadstairs for a few days. So I was at last becoming quite sociable.

Our new location turned out to be a good move, the neighbours being very friendly and supportive. Our immediate neighbours were a family of five – Wilf and Babs Newton, and their three daughters, Pamela, Jennifer and Shirley, who was the youngest. The girls were always in and out of our house, especially Jennifer, who was my special friend, and who often took care of me if my parents wanted to go out.

Just as things were settling down, Nana was rushed to hospital in December 1956, having suffered a brain haemorrhage. Mother and Father sat at her bedside and she came round for a short time, before slipping into a deep coma. My Mother was so distressed that my Father brought her home and tried to get her to rest. I know that she relied on Nana to help with me, and they were very close.

As I mentioned earlier in this book, Father had a strange experience when his brother died. Now the same thing happened to my Mother. She had gone to lie down in bed, feeling upset, and suddenly saw a disc of light move across the ceiling. Father remembers her sitting up in bed and saying that her Mother had just died, and that her spirit was leaving. Minutes later the telephone rang. It was Grandad, breaking the news that Nana had just died. We all felt desperate. Mother, in particular, felt absolutely lost.

My Father's family business continued as usual, and my Father carried on with his photographic modelling. I took virtually all Mother's time, but without Nana to help, our relationship became much closer. I was totally dependent on my parents; they were the only ones who could help me and I tried so hard to communicate something. A feeling of deep respect grew between us and I felt Mother's love become stronger. She used to say that her goal was to help me grow into a whole person and let me develop my mind as much as possible, to in some way compensate for being trapped in this body. Everyone tried so hard to explain things to me, to tell me what was going on, even though they had no idea how much I understood, if anything. I had to accept everything my parents gave me to eat or drink, for as my Father said, 'We don't even know whether Gail likes sugar!' They told me when someone knocked at the door, and who the person was. With such sensitive hearing, but with no speech or sight, every noise frightened me.

Life went on, but every time there was a chance of seeing someone who could help me, off we went to another hospital. The Social Services arranged an appointment at Great Ormond Street Hospital with the head child psychologist, who would assess my IQ. Once again we had nothing but a head-on collision with prejudice, negativity and a complete lack of compassion. They put me on a wooden chair with no arm rests, at a small table. Being seated on such a chair always made me feel very insecure, and I cried. On the table was a model village and the psychologist told me to pick up some little trees, and place them where I thought they ought to go. I'm blind, for goodness sake! Mother tried to interrupt to explain, but she was ignored. So I was assessed as a cabbage who would remain so for the rest of her life, and should be put into a home. I am glad this did not happen; even the experts can be wrong, and my case proved that you must never give up hope.

By this time it was 1957 and my parents decided that it would be nice to have a pet. So we purchased a St Bernard puppy, and called her Tina. She came from Winchester and was only four weeks old. She soon settled in and became a real member of the family. It may interest you to know that instructions for her care from the breeder included a note which said we should put an alarm clock under her blanket in the dog basket, so that she thought it was her Mother's heartbeat! My Father used to exercise her by walking her to the station every morning when he went to catch his train to London. My Mother would then drive down to the station in the car to pick her up, much to the amusement of the neighbours.

Some afternoons my Mother and I used to go to Kelsey Park, I in my pram, and Tina walking alongside. Often on our return journey Tina would feign fatigue, so my Mother would help her into the foot of my pram. At that time Tina was only three months old, but even then she was the size of a labrador, and she took up more than her fair share of the pram! My Mother soon got wise to this 'con-trick', and as she worried that I might be squashed, Tina was soon made to walk the full distance.

Ever since then we have had a dog, but I have to be honest and say that I don't particularly like stroking them – why, I don't know.

About this time my parents bought me a tricycle, and

put leather straps on the pedals to secure my feet as they kept slipping off. This helped stretch my legs and I managed to turn the pedals round, and with either my Mother or Father to hold me steady and to guide me, I was able to move around.

Meanwhile I had made some other new friends. There was a pub in Addington called The Cricketers, where the landlord and his family became good friends. They used to have me over to stay, and I loved to play an old bongo drum behind the bar, in time to the background music. There was still no speech, but I proved I had a sense of rhythm. My Father tried to encourage me to talk by sitting down after lunch and offering me some chocolate. He used to say 'Gail say "yes" ', or 'Gail say "tes" '. Nothing happened. He recognises now that it was so upsetting for me, as I could not, for whatever reason, say 'yes'. In desperation I began to bite the flesh on my hands and arms. The wounds bled, and it was agony, but I was so frustrated I couldn't get through to anyone. I just did not know what to do with myself. Mother refused to accept that my silence was part of my general condition and over-all handicap, and decided that we had to sort things out once and for all. So an appointment was made at the Croydon Spastics Centre for me to be again 'assessed'.

We arrived, and were shown into a room where a consultant, a physiotherapist, a teacher and a speech therapist sat. As usual, I started to disrupt the proceedings, but my Mother managed to quieten me, and show the committee that I understood what was said to me, by demonstrating my ability to differentiate the shapes on the pegboard, and by counting them.

The speech therapist, Miss Leather, said she would like to try and help me. My parents were both relieved and excited, as was I.

My Father remembers Miss Leather as being very

attractive, bubbly and a lovely person. She was also brimming with confidence. She never suggested at any time that I would not or could not talk. Initially, all she did was to gain my trust. Yes, there was a screaming session, but she ignored it and accepted it without question or comment. So I stopped doing it, and we then got on like a house on fire. After about four visits Miss Leather asked my Mother to leave us alone. I know Mother was a bit apprehensive, but she decided to let Miss Leather have me to herself.

I was frightened, and the only way we could communicate was to give each other taps on the hand. I could understand what she said to me, but I couldn't reply. What Miss Leather did next was to put her fingers in my mouth and make the right shape for sounds like 'MMMM' or 'BBBB'. After the first five sessions we were off! I soon learned to say Mother and Father and after that there was no stopping me. At last I could communicate and say what I wanted, what I needed. Thank goodness I never gave up hope, and neither did Miss Leather, because, let me tell you, there always has to be hope. I was nine years old, and I could talk.

What Miss Leather did was so simple, but it worked. It shows that what I had was an emotional or mental blockage with speech, and it just needed someone with expert experience to believe in me and to give me the confidence to try. A whole new world opened up.

Over the years my speech has improved, although if I get very excited, it can go a bit haywire. But the fact of the matter is that I overcame everything except for a slight impediment which is connected with the cerebral palsy, and after all the doctors' negativity, and in spite of it, I proved that I am intelligent.

My new-found ability to communicate enabled the family to function as near normal as possible, and I can

27

assure you it was a great relief to everyone. Physically I was very limited and was carried everywhere until I got my wheelchair at the age of nine. The tension seemed to lift and my parents began to remember amusing incidents, rather than just sad ones.

I know that my Mother and Father think we were extremely lucky to meet Miss Leather. She changed our lives like magic.

6

In late 1959, my parents wondered if there was any chance of extending our family so that I would have brothers and sisters to keep me company. Mother went off to see her specialist, but sadly, she was told she couldn't have any more children. She has a rare problem, in that her womb is actually split into two halves. This is the reason I was born after only 26 weeks and there was little chance of carrying a baby full-term. She didn't know this when she had me, but felt that she couldn't risk another handicapped baby. So, adoption or fostering was considered. My Father had great ideas of creating a large family, where we could form our own band and he could teach the boys cricket and they could enter the family business, but after visiting the adoption societies, he came away empty-handed. Bad luck for us and bad luck for them. It could have been great. But as neither option worked out, I was to remain the one and only child.

For company, my Mother started to take me to the Croydon Spastic Centre and we often stopped at the pub in Addington to help with lunches. This sparked the thought that it might be an idea to buy a pub or hotel so that my parents could spend more time with me and my Father could be around to help during the day. They heard of a small place in Tenby, South Wales, and my Father duly went off to have a look, with Geraint Evans for company and support. They met up with his brother-in-law, Glynn Davies, a Welsh international rugby player. The hotel wasn't up to much and not worth pursuing, but from what I heard, they had a wonderful weekend. Can you just imagine the three of them? My Father, a Welsh rugby player and an opera singer in Wales!

The previous summer, my Father had played cricket for the Licensed Victuallers team. The wicketkeeper was a regional manager from Charringtons Brewery and he was able to offer help in finding a local pub. The Bull at Chelsham, near Warlingham, was suggested. With no hot water and draughts coming from every nook and cranny, there was only one way for it to go and that was upwards. The rent was £180 a year; by the time we were ready to move on after six years the brewery had increased the rent to £5,000. In other words it was a huge success. But it needed a lot of work and to give some idea of what we moved into, the previous landlady insisted on leaving a wardrobe in one bedroom. Not wanting it, my parents heaved it out of the way only to find a huge hole, giving them a perfect bird's eye view of the bar below.

The pub had to be occupied within three months and we moved in just before Christmas 1960. I had to remain with neighbours for a week as I had bronchitis. The occasion was marked by a lovely piece in the paper all about me. That year the *People* newspaper published on Christmas Day, and on the front page was a photo of me, opening presents, as part of an appeal for blind children. I must have touched a lot of people, because the full amount of £30,000 (possibly equivalent to £300,000 today) was raised within days, with hundreds of letters offering help.

However, back to the pub. My parents had no experience of running a pub, so by all accounts, it was a brave decision for them to have taken. But everything they have done has been with me in mind and they have never been afraid to take a risk. The brewery cellar inspector gave a crash course in how to keep the beer in good condition. Fortunately, Mother seemed to have a natural gift and the pub soon became very popular. A group of regulars established itself and the public bar was always full. My Father reckons most of them had actually done time, but they were wonderfully protective of the family and thought the world of me, even guiding me around the car park on my tricycle at weekends.

Meanwhile, Mother was anxious to get on with improving the pub and turned the lounge bar into a restaurant. My Father pitched in full-time, as the family business, which he had struggled with for so long, was sold off. The pub flourished and on a Sunday morning there were over 100 cars in the car park. We could sell 72 gallons of bitter (about 600 pints) in the morning. The clientele improved and The Bull attracted celebrities of the day, like Derek Roy, David Hemmings, Tim Gudgeon and the singer Michael Holliday. My Father remembers Michael being in the pub just a couple of nights before he died by his own hand. At a local charity concert they sat together and he recalls Mr Holliday saying how nervous he was just before singing, and of course he had such a lovely voice. His death was tragic.

Mother's beer gained quite a reputation. She learned how to take the beer engines and pumps to pieces and, from a cellar full of green slime and frogs, she made it immaculate. We soon gained a reputation for serving good food as well. According to my Father's memory, the only way he got fed each night was to place an order, and as a steak sandwich appeared, grab a table and enjoy it! As you have probably gathered my parents were good hosts. They are outgoing people and always entered into the spirit of things. On St Patrick's Day they would put crates of

Guinness on the counter so that the customers could help themselves, and my Father tells me he used to wear a green sweater and shamrock for effect; if you can't beat them, join them. As the business prospered we got a second-hand Rolls Royce, which was used to take the regulars round to local darts matches on a Friday night – then the public bar customers spent all Sunday morning cleaning the car.

It was hectic living at The Bull, but things were going in the right direction. I sat in the kitchen and the staff paid a lot of attention to me. Betty, one of the helpers, shared a bedroom with me. She was also a riding instructor at the Selsdon Park Hotel, so I did a bit of riding, held in the saddle by Betty and my Father. Riding is good for disabled people as it lets you feel the movement of the horse. Swimming is another enjoyable exercise; water is lovely for me to move in, because I feel free. Sometimes, if we can borrow a private pool, we take a cassette machine and dance in the water!

I love showjumping on the TV and was thrilled to bits when I got my own horse. One evening a friend mentioned to my Father, at a benefit dance for the Surrey and England cricketer Tony Lock, that he was having one of his horses at the riding stables put down. The horse, called Major, was suffering from ringbone and was really too old to ride. Father, being the sort of person he is, offered £50 to save Major from being shot. He was duly delivered to us the following morning. We had to turn the Rolls out into the open so that the garage could become a stable. A huge cob, an ex-baker's horse, he spent his last ten years as part of the family.

There was still concern over my education, or rather lack of it. I went to school at the Spastics Centre, and enjoyed being in plays, because I was the only one in the class who could remember the lines. My Father took me to school, the hours being 9.00 a.m. to 3.30 p.m. At first I stayed all day, but I hated the school dinners. It was here that the matron told me that we were having steak for the meal. Now I had eaten steak, and knew the taste, and this was not steak. I was eventually told that it was liver, which I dislike. It was very confusing, and very wrong to try and mislead a blind person in this way. From then on I came home for lunch.

Around this time we went to visit the Sunshine Home in East Grinstead. It was lovely there, and I remember a kind lady called Miss Clark. She was really nice to me. We often used to drive down to the Felbridge Hotel at East Grinstead if the weather was good, and we could find time. On one of these occasions it was the meeting of the Guinea Pig Club (a club formed for severely burnt Second World War servicemen) and I was having a swim in the pool with my parents. There were a number of famous names amongst the members, including James Wright, a severely disfigured ex-RAF pilot, who was also blind. His nurse/companion told him about me, and he asked that we might be introduced. He was a lovely person, interesting and witty, and we got on well together.

Also at the hotel was Max Bygraves, who spoke to me. I told him I did not approve of his bad grammar in the song *'Fings Ain't What They Used to Be'*. He apologised but said that he didn't think he would have sold many copies if he had changed the words.

7

I was much happier than I had been in years. My parents still wanted me to be better educated, and so set about finding private tutors.

A local lady, Mrs Mattingley, agreed to take me for French twice a week, and my Father drove me over to her house. She was an ex-grammar school teacher, with a spastic daughter of her own. We often had lunch together. Mrs Mattingley also looked after her Mother, who had senile dementia, and for some reason I was the only person who could calm her down when she began to rant.

Another teacher was found for English and history, and it was she who spotted my amazing memory. She would read a poem, which I could then recite back to her, perfectly, after just the one hearing.

The teacher at the Croydon Spastics Centre was preparing a Christmas concert, and as I and a boy called Graham Burn (who later went on to Whitgift School) were the only two who could talk reasonably well, we were given poems to recite. The teacher, Mrs Coleman, decided that I would recite a poem called 'The Lone Dog', a very long piece. She read it to me and said that she would ask my parents to take the poem home and teach it to me.

'Why do you want me to take it home?' I said. 'You have read it to me, so now I can recite it.' Which I did! Mrs

Coleman was stunned – it was the first time I had the chance to prove my excellent powers of memory.

Mrs Caspar, my English and history teacher, was convinced I was a reincarnation of William Shakespeare, as I could quote the words from '*As You Like It*', before she read them. Actually, I had heard the play on the radio – just once!

Piano lessons with a Mrs Mepphen followed, and after all the brickbats of the first ten years it was time for some bouquets. I have perfect pitch; that is to say I could, and still can, identify the key of any piece of music being played. Sadly, the actual playing of the piano proved to be very hard for me because of the stiffness in my fingers, caused, of course by my spastic condition. In fact it is really only my right arm and hand which work well. Any thoughts of a musical career came to an end, but as an interest it has brought me a lot of happiness. My teacher told my Father that in her opinion I had as much music in my head as Beethoven, if only it could be brought out. My Father thought she was joking, but she insisted that she was quite serious.

I listen to the radio for hours. One of my favourite singers is Nat King Cole. He put such feeling into his songs, and he had a warmth in his voice all his own. When he sang 'Let there be love', he meant it. Matt Munro was the same. Since we are talking about music here, my favourite song is Louis Armstrong's *What a Wonderful World*. It says everything.

One day a regular customer, Vivien Batchelor, a journalist with the *Evening Standard*, came into the pub. She was on her way to interview Mrs Wilson, wife of the then Prime Minister, at Number 10. Father suggested that she leave politics alone and write about the scandal of Surrey Education Authority not helping with my education. The spastic schools would not help, because of my blindness,

35

and vice versa with the blind schools. Viv was quite horrified, and duly wrote an article in the *Evening Standard*.

As if by magic, the head of the Surrey Education Board appeared on our doorstep, almost immediately thereafter. His first move was to approach me without a word, and blow a whistle in my ear. I jumped out of my skin with shock. My Father asked him why he had done this, and was told it was to see if I was deaf. 'Couldn't you have asked her?' said my Father. It was downhill all the way from there.

A discussion on the merits of educating me followed. My Father asked him what he considered was the purpose of education, and received the reply 'To feed the mind.' 'Why do you want her educated?' the gentleman then asked my Father.

'Why do you educate other children?'

'To feed their minds,' he repeated.

'Don't you think Gail's mind needs feeding more than most? I'm beginning to think that it is you who needs the education, not Gail.'

Like so many others, he treated me as if I was not there. But I was, and still am!

Eventually, the agreement was reached that if my parents could find tutors, then Surrey Education would help to pay for them. The only concession was that a Braille teacher be found by the council. This teacher came round for about six months, and then abandoned the project, saying I would never learn Braille because I could not follow a straight line with my finger. My sensory perception is badly impaired. For example, I cannot touch my nose with my finger first go.

Both my parents felt that there was little concern on the part of the authorities, and they had to fight every inch of the way on my behalf in the belief that not only was I worth it, but that I had every right to achieve my potential whatever that might be. Yes, I am disabled, but I do not think that anything has held me back, because I will not let it. You simply have to work with what you've got.

8

It was 1963 and, having settled down to pub life, we all decided it was time for a holiday. Since I had never flown, the island of Jersey was chosen, being only an hour's flight. By this time my epilepsy had more or less stopped, and with improving health everything was much easier.

As soon as one of the ground staff at Gatwick Airport spotted my wheelchair, what I can only describe as VIP treament began. We were escorted to a private lounge and allowed on to the plane before anyone else. I have no sense of motion. For example, in a lift I cannot tell whether it's travelling up or down, so Mother kept up a running commentary on what was happening as it was all new to me. The flight was very good, the landing was smooth and, it may interest you to know, I gave the pilot a sweet to show my appreciation.

I received the same VIP treatment on landing in Jersey. British Caledonian, as it was then, had arranged for one of the staff to meet me on the tarmac with a wheelchair, and a taxi was waiting outside the arrivals lounge.

The holiday was a great success and this was due in part to the fact that people were so helpful. At the Hotel Ambassadeur in St Clements Bay there was another warm welcome, when the resident pianist even stayed on late in the restaurant to play during our evening meal when all the other guests had departed. He really made a fuss of me and played a favourite tune of mine, the old Nat King Cole song '*Unforgettable*'. The pianist also amused me no end by playing the wrong notes – deliberately! One of the guests a Vince Coulson from Doncaster, also helped to make the holiday extra special by being a constant companion and by holding out a hand of friendship. Whenever we went out, he came as well. My Father hired a taxi each day for trips around the island and the driver kept telling me I was in the same seat as John Lennon had been. Apparently, he had driven the Beatles around Jersey. The week ended all too soon, but I have very happy memories of that holiday.

It was back to work at The Bull until our next holiday in 1965. This time we stayed on mainland Britain. It was a complete contrast to the lovely experience in Jersey. My parents booked a suite in a hotel in Sidmouth, Devon. The restaurant manager made it quite clear that we were not welcome to eat with the other guests by suggesting that the meals were delivered to our suite. He actually said, 'I'll have your meals sent up to your room. It will be more convenient.' My Father stood his ground and refused. I can eat unaided with my fingers and I am not an embarrassment. One of the waiters, a Spaniard named José, was the only considerate person. When I was wheeled into the restaurant he would announce, 'The princess has arrived. Everyone else must wait! For you, today, princess, I have some beautiful breast of chicken! For your Father, some sparrow's kneecaps!' The other guests were amused by all this and it was just the management who seemed to think it was a problem. It was all unnecessary. I don't need to be segregated, just included in life, like everyone else.

José even offered to take me out in his car on his day off, but as it appeared to be held together with string, my Father declined the offer.

Back home there were frequent trips to the stables at the neighbouring Selsdon Park Hotel. Riding was still good exercise for me because it made me use my leg muscles and, as explained, it gave me a sense of freedom beyond that experienced in the confines of the wheelchair. I was very settled at this point, having developed a good friendship with Betty, my room-mate, and we would talk or listen to the radio until the early hours of the morning – until my Father came in to tell us to go to sleep!

The next high point, quite out of the blue, was that my Father decided to be christened. Unusual at his age – he was 40 – but he felt it was something that he wanted to do. He thought perhaps it could be combined with confirmation and approached the local vicar, who understood the confirmation, but was surprised at the christening. Religious instruction classes followed and he was duly christened at Warlingham, Surrey, with Mother as his Godmother. The confirmation by the Bishop of Woolwich followed at Limpsfield along with 30 school-girls. Quite an experience. We have a strong faith and there is no doubt that this helps carry us through the difficult times – but more of this later.

The pub was doing well, and, as already explained, my Father, the 'Guvnor', had a Rolls Royce. The public bar regulars still washed and polished it, taking their shoes off before they got into it. Mother had a Triumph Roadster by this time, but it was not in particularly good shape, so it was sold by Len Ward, the Father of the actor, Simon Ward of *Young Winston* fame, and many other starring roles. Len said that he was probably the greatest car salesman in the world, but he doubted whether even he was good enough to sell this car, but eventually he did.

Prior to this sale, my Father used to put our horse Major on the car park when the snow was around, with a bundle of hay, and one Sunday morning some customers told him that the horse was eating the soft top of my Mother's car. Thinking that they were pulling his leg, he said, 'Oh yes, he has one every Sunday.' When he strolled outside later the horse had stripped the roof bare!

Tina, our St Bernard, had taken well to pub life, as she had a lovely temperament. Unfortunately everyone used to spoil her and feed her sausages, and consequently she became very fat. When she was ten years old, during a very hot summer, she had a heart attack. Mother packed ice around her head and neck – so there was no ice for drinks that Saturday night. The customers were all very understanding, as they knew Tina as a fund-raiser for charity, and was a loveable character. No one complained, but unfortunately she passed away peacefully in the early hours of Sunday morning.

My family do not like being without a dog, and my parents thought they would like an Old English Mastiff, but we preferred not to have a puppy, which would require training. We then heard of a young mastiff whom the breeder was intending to keep for showing. He was six months old, very large and well proportioned, but what the breeder omitted to tell us was that his eyesight was very poor, which we only realised later. The breeder brought him by train to St Pancras station, where my Father picked him up. Our new puppy was very nervous, which made it difficult for my Father during his drive home. He was named Simba.

The years passed by, and in 1966 my parents thought it time to move on, to be able to spend more time with me, and to find a nicer environment for me to live in. Having made quite a success in the hospitality industry, an hotel seemed to be the next step forward.

9

My parents began to look at properties in Brighton, Eastbourne and Midhurst. Money was a major factor and for a while nothing seemed to be in their price range.

One day, on the return trip from another fruitless search on the South Coast, they passed the Bramley Grange Hotel, just three miles from Guildford on the Horsham road. Mother made the comment, 'I like the look of that.' Two weeks later she was browsing through *The Caterer Magazine*. Almost unbelievably, in the October edition the Bramley Grange Hotel was advertised as being for sale! And it had a paddock for Major. The asking price was double what they could afford but they made an offer anyway.

The owner, Mrs Gordon, was very keen to sell to a family, as opposed to a large chain or hotel group, which would not have kept it quite so personal. My Father met her early one afternoon and they talked for about an hour. He put forward his proposals. It was obvious that with other interested parties coming up with the asking price, his chances were less than slim. He came home, not feeling very hopeful. Then the phone rang. It was Mrs Gordon's solicitor. Against all the odds the offer was accepted, providing my Father could complete before Christmas. Mrs Gordon's husband had died the previous

December and she did not want to be running the Bramley Grange at the anniversary of his death.

From what I am told, Mrs Gordon was very kind to my parents. I think she wanted them to have the hotel and she bent over backwards to help them.

My parents remember the bank being sympathetic, agreeing that it looked a good deal and appearing to be generally co-operative, although the manager did say that because of a credit squeeze, there was no guarantee that the loan would be authorised. My Father visited Bramley Grange several times for talks with Mrs Gordon, but it was obvious that he was quite worried. At this stage I had not been to the hotel and it was all a bit unsettling. The weeks passed by and there was no news from the bank. My Father went alone to London to sign the exchange of contracts, which his solicitor advised against because, without the money, he could have been in a lot of trouble. He signed the papers, got in the car to drive home, and it may interest you to know, he was physically sick, on the way, from worry. But he would do anything to help make my life more comfortable and to work towards financial security.

It was now mid-December and still there was no news. With just ten days to go before completion the bank rang to say that the loan had been agreed. My Father was over the moon, laughed and was so relieved he wanted to kiss the manager down the phone. But they were not quite out of the woods yet. There was a shortfall of several thousand pounds. A wealthy family friend chipped in £5,000 and, can you believe it, so did I, or rather my piggy bank – for the last £19. Completion was on 21 December 1966.

Although my parents' decision to move had been made with the best of intentions, so as to give me a better life, I didn't react very well to the news. Change was very hard because it unsettled me. I had made lots of friends and was

43

very happy at The Bull, so I hope you will understand and not think too badly of me when I say that I was sad, very sad, to be leaving the pub. But when my Father sat down and explained the reasons to me, I soon began to think that, given time, I'd like my new home – although when the day came, I have to say that it was a bit traumatic. You know, it is surprising how attached you can get to people and places. I dreaded leaving Betty, even though she was going to join us eventually at the Bramley Grange. She had to stay and run the pub until our lease expired and the business was formally handed over to the new tenants. We also had to leave our new pet, Simba, behind, until we had settled in the hotel. Of course, Christmas was no time to cope with him, because he had bad eyesight and my Mother says he was neurotic.

Mother and Father sent a manager (who had previously been engaged to help at The Bull) ahead to get the feel for the new place. Although we all remember him quite fondly, he nearly came to grief before moving to the hotel. It may interest you to know that he had been taken prisoner by the Japanese in the war and often went back to his room late at night to drink, presumably to block out the memories. He used to make a supper of Stilton cheese on toast with curry powder. It used to smell awful! One night he fell asleep – well, sort of unconscious, actually. The story goes that he had a lighted cigarette in his hand which dropped on to the carpet. Smoke billowed out from under his door, but fortunately Mother and Father were able to put out the fire and rescue their would be manager. Talk about going out in a blaze!

Just four days before Christmas, my parents packed up the car and we set off on our journey to the Grange, across the county of Surrey. I was so upset at the move I could not stop crying, and, I'm sorry to say, I was sick in the car. I suffered from awful carsickness. Within five minutes of starting a journey, I would be sick. This usual sickness was made worse by my upset at moving. You may think, how lucky to have a Rolls, but I must say that the firm ride of a Ford Popular suited me much better.

Eventually we arrived in Bramley and Mother and Father proudly took over a prestigious, Victorian-built country house hotel, set in 20 acres of gardens and woodland. It had 36 bedrooms, but no one had remembered to reserve one for us! And, it being Christmas, the hotel was full. So the first night was spent with two in a single bed, with a put-you-up for the third person in the corner, and no private bathroom. Not exactly comfortable.

Our horse Major had been brought from The Bull, but he also found that he was not able to stay at the hotel. The adjoining paddock was being let to a local riding stable, so he was billeted in a field in Shalford, a neighbouring village. The weather was dreadful, and Mother and Father felt they could not leave him out there on his own, so they acquired a horsebox, and in the pouring rain they cajoled and coaxed him into the box and brought him home. Mother's new suede jacket was ruined, and she had just had her hair done for Christmas as well!

Soon thereafter, they made a stable for him in the yard, near the kitchens, piled in lots of straw, built a feeding shelf and installed electric lighting. It was very cosy. Early each morning Mother mucked out and the gardener used to lead him up to the paddock. Major had a happy final few years.

You often hear people say, 'Aren't so and so lucky, it never happens to us.' Well, despite all these early problems, as far as my Father was concerned, he had been very lucky, and it had happened to us. He would walk round the gardens every morning and say to himself, 'You are a lucky devil, Taylor!'

10

As the new owners, the first priority was to meet the staff at the Christmas party, and I accompanied my parents. It was at this party that I met Ethel Hudson, who by this time had been at the Bramley Grange for 36 years, doing every conceivable job, and was well into her sixties. From what friends and local people recall, Ethel (nicknamed 'Lethal' by my Father, much to Ethel's amusement) first came to the Grange in 1930 as a 'temp' from the Alfred Marks Employment Bureau. It must be one of their longest placements!

She married Dick Hudson, the hotel's chauffeur, and they lived just across the road on the site of what is now a filling station. She passed away a few years ago, but I remember her with a lot of love and affection, because although she could be a bit possessive and protective of me, she became my very best friend. We would sit together when she had finished her bar duties. We watched a lot of racing on television, and that is how I came to know about all the horses, jockeys, and trainers. We also liked watching the comedy and quiz series.

Ethel had lunch with me in the restaurant two or three times a week. It was always very pleasant and enjoyable. I like a good steak, pork and meat dishes in general. I try to keep a balanced diet and I don't eat chips or chocolates –

much as I like them. I try to avoid sweet things because of my weight, but I eat lots of fruit and vegetables. I never eat or drink between meals. How's that for healthy self-discipline!

While on the subject of health, I have always had physiotherapy each week, and on moving to the Bramley Grange I was able to go for treatment to Unstead Park, a private rehabilitation centre, which is less than a mile from the hotel. The staff certainly put me through it, pulling and stretching me all over the place. One of the physiotherapists used to play hockey for England, and was she strong! I exercised in the swimming pool, and as I have mentioned, one of my favourite things is to dance in the water with my Father. It is not easy to keep in tip-top health, for obvious reasons, but I try hard. I am told that I have a good clear skin, and take great pride in my appearance. I love a long relaxing wallow in the bath.

After we arrived at the Grange it was very important to my Mother to find a good doctor. We registered with the established village practice, about a hundred yards from us, a husband-and-wife team. As we became more established at the hotel, my Mother was keen to find a younger doctor more in tune with my needs. She got in touch with a fairly new practice at Wonersh (a nearby village), and explained the situation.

Dr Ian Hatrick (who had recently joined the practice), a charming, good-looking, dark-haired young man, came to see me, and we immediately hit it off. He even offered to brush up his French with me. We became real friends and I loved him very much. He was always there for me, and Diana, his wife, also became a friend. Tragically, three years ago he was diagnosed as having cancer. After a major operation and chemotherapy, he bravely returned to the practice for a short while, but his illness forced him to retire, and he died at home on 12 June 1995. He is still sadly missed by all his patients. We all went to his funeral service at Wonersh. The church was overflowing, but his family had saved a space for my wheelchair.

Diana took the trouble to write to me the day before the funeral, and her letter is reproduced opposite.

We all wondered who would replace Ian. We, and I am sure all his patients, were apprehensive, thinking that no one could match him, and we had to wait three months before his successor was announced. It was Dr Shaun O'Hanlon. About a month after he was appointed I went down with a tummy virus. Such problems are particularly unpleasant for me, as I cannot get to the toilet in time, when necessary, despite my parents' best efforts. Dr O'Hanlon was called, and we were delighted to meet him. He immediately sat down with me and put me at my ease – just as Ian had done. He came over as a very friendly, caring person, and I knew at once that I was extremely lucky to have him as a doctor. As Ian had done, he gave my Father his home number, and said that if my parents were ever worried about me they should phone, and he would come out. It was a great relief and joy to us all that Ian's successor was to also become my friend, as well as my physician.

My Mother also found a super dental surgeon, Robert Jones, who lived in Bramley. His surgery was in nearby Godalming, on the first floor of a small building in a cul-de-sac, and impossible for me to negotiate. On one of my Mother's appointments with Mr Jones, she tentatively enquired whether he would be prepared to treat me, explaining my situation. Robert immediately agreed to take me on as a home visit patient. He has looked after me well for a number of years. I am probably his only patient who looks forward to his visits! His wife Liz has also become a friend, and they have four lovely daughters.

Meanwhile, my Mother and Father were getting on with

Eastwater House,
Snowdenham Lane,
Bramley, Surrey. GU5 0DB

13 · 6 · 95 .

Dear Ken, Pam & Gail.

My sister and brother-in-law
are popping in for dinner tonight
and I wanted them to drop this in for you.

You may have heard that poor Ian
died on Friday - very peacefully with
all his family with him at the end.

Please tell Gail that he derived
so much pleasure from listening to her
lovely tapes, whilst he sat in his chair
trying to forget the pain he was in. He
always admired Gail and used to love
seeing her.

The funeral is tomorrow at
midday and once that is over perhaps
I shall not feel quite so desolate.

Much love and see you soon
Diana.

the business of running the hotel. Mrs Gordon had organised the Christmas and New Year festivities, so we had time to gather ourselves together, and move into a suite on the ground floor overlooking the gardens. This was most suitable, bearing in mind that Simba, who would be rejoining us shortly, needed exercise.

When Simba came to us, he was fine with me, and very nice to Ethel and her miniature poodle BeeGee (named after the Bramley Grange). Ethel used to take both the dogs out for a walk. I believe she was only 4 feet 9 inches, and Simba, being such a large dog, made her look even smaller, but they got on very well. (Perhaps I should point out here that I cannot tell size, and have to rely on what I am told.) It may interest you to know that age and colour do not mean a lot to me. If someone is old, it means that they have lived a long time. I remember a Mrs Von Der Hyde, who, I am told, was 87, saying to me, 'You see, Gail, I am very old,' and I replied, 'You're not old, Vondy, you've just lived a long time.' She wasn't old to me, she had a very young outlook on life. The same with coloured people, I have no prejudice about colour. Everybody is the same colour to me. They are nice or not so nice; I judge on the personality of people.

Mrs Gordon had decided not to leave the hotel immediately and stayed for 18 months, using the hotel as her home, and she dined each evening in the restaurant with us.

Every Saturday there was a dinner dance, and I loved to listen to the music. I began to settle down again, but it was hard work for my parents, 14 hours a day, 7 days a week, and living in meant they were permanently on call. But life had definitely taken a turn for the better.

My Mother got involved in the business very quickly, while Father dealt with a lot of the administration, banking and paying wages. The manager left, and there was a bit of tightening up to do with the reception staff, who had previously been allowed to eat in the restaurant and more or less ask for anything they wanted. Mother soon put a stop to this practice, along with the under manager leaving his shoes out at night to be cleaned. Then in the storeroom she was horrified to find four sacks of dried peas, enough tinned potatoes and vegetables for a 12-month siege, not to mention 54 pounds of lentils. She was not content with offering anything other than fresh food – this was a three-star hotel – so the contents of the storeroom were returned to the wholesalers. We soon found out that Mrs Gordon had taken little part in the running of the hotel – leaving it to her manager.

It was all change in the hotel as Mother's new broom swept through. She had difficulties in the restaurant, as most of the staff were Spanish. She thought most of them were related to Manuel out of *Fawlty Towers* and very few spoke English, although they were willing enough. The chambermaids were wives of the Spanish waiters and they got more and more greedy, so she found some local housewives instead.

My parents were both deeply involved in the running of the hotel as all our finances were tied up in this venture. It was a new learning experience for them because it was a very different life from the pub, where Mother cooked, served and looked after the cellar. Now, if one chef or the other walked out there was nothing to do but turn her hand to running the kitchens. She enjoyed cooking in moderation, but this was not really her scene; it was extremely hard work, hot and stressful, to get the orders out on time, cooked to perfection.

By now I had settled quite well and at noon every day, I was wheeled into the kitchen to help with the washing-up, just drying a few pots, while listening to the radio. I also kept the air pure. The chefs were more restrained with

51

their language when I was around, so the air was much less blue.

Having already passed the GCE O level, I continued my French lessons at Woldingham with Mrs Mattingley as she was very keen for me to take a Chamber of Commerce exam in French and thought I had a good chance of passing. An adjudicator came to the hotel from Oxford to test me. The lady was herself French, and regretted that 10 per cent of the maximum marks would have to be deducted, as I was unable to do the written part. However, I managed to obtain 89 per cent, so in fact only dropped one mark.

Mrs Mattingley had by then, unfortunately, taken me as far as she was able, so my tutoring continued at Guildford. My next tutor was a Mr Fillingham, who taught languages at the Guildford Technical College. He was so keen that he taught me advanced French and German without speaking a word of English, and we progressed like a house on fire. Unfortunately, he left the college for another post, and a Professor Heyman took his place to continue my French. I also had a tutor for Italian for a short time, which I also enjoyed learning.

My Spanish, Portuguese and Italian were taught mostly by various members of the staff working at the hotel. I found that languages are my forte, and I really enjoy learning and speaking them. I was lucky to have the opportunity to practise. As I have already mentioned, everyone is always so willing to help me, and my Mother has always encouraged me to strive, within my limitations, for goals that other people could not achieve.

The year 1972 was important for me because in the October I was 21. Beautiful invitations were printed, with gold lettering. Mother and Father shut the restaurant and we had a brilliant dinner with a band, a jukebox and 80 guests. I really enjoyed that and Sir Geraint Evans my god-father, came. One of the nicest photos I have showing

Sir Geraint and myself together was taken on that evening. It may interest you to know that even the local dustmen came, together with old friends from The Bull at Warlingham. My Father sent a coach over for them! All the flower arrangements were done by a friend called Ann Bradley and she had blue-tinted carnations flown in specially, because she knew that blue was my favourite colour.

11

Not long after that, I spent my first nights away from home, ever. This adventure was arranged by an organisation called PHAB, which stands for Physically Handicapped and Able Bodied. Its aims are to 'promote and encourage people with and without physical disabilities to come together on equal terms; to achieve complete integration within the wider community'. One of my tutors mentioned it to me and I was excited at the possibility of outings.

I know my parents were worried about me. They took me to Cranleigh School, where the course was being held, and my Father says he came back and just waited for someone to phone and say I was homesick and wanted to come home. But I didn't. We had a Spanish waiter who worked at the school during the day and who used to give my Mother and Father a report on how I was getting on. I think they really missed me. The hotel staff said that they were unbearable and my Father got rheumatism in his shoulder where Mother had made it damp, crying herself to sleep every night I was away.

I went to the cinema, theatre and to Brighton, and went in the swimming pool. The sixth-form boys used to queue up to kiss me goodnight. It was wonderful.

Meanwhile the tourist trade was good and there was a

My mother and father getting married, 1951 (page 8)

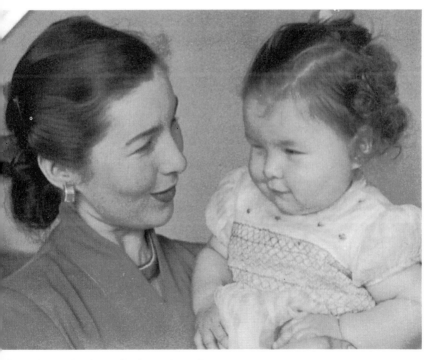

Gail with her mother in our first house (page 9)

On holiday at Pevensey, Mother, Father and Gail (page 19)

Family outside new house in Park Langley, Beckenham (page 23)

Family with Tina, the St. Bernard, in Kelsey Park (page 25)

No. 4125
80th Year
4D.

Sunday, December 25, 1960

THE PEOPLE

THE PAPER THAT LOOKS AHEAD

Read this to the family

A LITTLE blind girl opens her first Christmas presents. Her groping hands tell her all she wants to know. Her eyes are closed but her face lights up with joy. . . .

A middle-aged man plays Father Christmas to a bunch of delighted youngsters, and it's plain to see that he is as happy as they are. . . .

We want you to remember them both today and when you know why, we feel sure you will.

For the Father Christmas is Gilbert Harding. It was a picture taken four years ago—and how he enjoyed himself with the youngsters that day.

This Christmas he was planning to make an appeal to "People" readers for £30,000, so that he could help a dozen good causes, including little girls like Gail Taylor.

You see her in the top picture. She is a blind spastic, home for Christmas from the spinal spastic school she attends.

Gilbert Harding is gone and so, in his memory, "The People" is trying to raise the £30,000 he wanted for them.

Would you help by making a collection around the family after dinner today? Please do—and then turn to Page Five to see where to send the money. . . . In memory of Gilbert's good works and in tribute to Gail's courage.

The People published a front page photograph of Gail on Christmas Day, 1960 (page 30)

beer advert. Outside the Bull in Chesham. Mother and Father, Betty in background (page 30)

Dancing in the water with my father at Unsted Park (page 47)

Gail and Sir Geraint. Gail's 21st birthday (page 52)

…ail, Ann Bradley, Ethel and Mother at 'Miss World' Contest (page 62)

…eft to right: Bobby Short, Robin Short, Rita Short, Carole Smythe, Len Crane, Linda Short,
…rna and Kevin' at a Bramley Grange Hotel dinner dance (page 68)

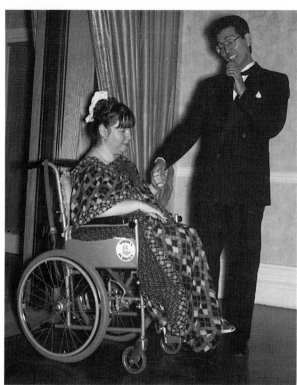

Gail with Johnny Camark
the Japanese Frank Sinatr
serenading Gail (page 69)

Tony Evans, orchestra leader,
and Gail (page 69)

Phil Bailey of Earth, Wind and Fire with Gail and her friend Beth (page 74)

...il's confirmation. Clockwise from left: Phil Bailey, Lady Brenda Evans, Sir Geraint Evans, ...s. Brenda Evans and Bishop Kenneth Evans (no relation to Sir Geraint), Liz Farrell, ...aham Wylie, Ann Bradley, Rev. Tom Farrell, Pam Taylor, Gail, Ken Taylor, Joan Wylie ...age 75)

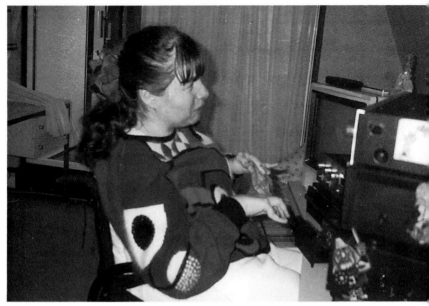

Gail at her radio equipment (page 100)

Our flat in the hotel, arrowed (page 109)

Our flat after the fire (page 109)

constant stream of visitors from the US, Canada, Holland and Japan, to mention a few countries. The Bramley Grange also had conference facilities, which were used by companies like IBM, Shell and BP. But, of most interest to me, were the celebrities. Guildford is only about three miles away and is proud to have the Yvonne Arnaud Theatre. But more of this later. Many guests were parents visiting their children at local public schools. The public schools of Cranleigh and Charterhouse, in Godalming, are within five miles, and St Catherine's School for Girls is just across the road from the hotel. A few of the sixth formers from there used to come over to tea, once a week, and I was allowed to sit in on the French lessons.

My parents continued aiming to maintain the high standard and international reputation of the hotel. This was not an easy task, as they lacked experience, and with a large bank loan to pay off, they could not really afford an experienced manager. My Mother had to turn her hand to doing all the jobs in the hotel, and 'fill in' where needed. It was very difficult at the time to get staff, apart from Spanish, Italian and Portuguese, who mostly spoke poor English – which situation, of course, helped me enormously with my learning of foreign languages!

My Mother worked very long hours, and I know that she worried about neglecting me, being torn between the necessities of running the hotel and putting the business on a profitable footing to pay back the money they had borrowed, and looking after me, which, as you will understand, was a full-time job, but the hotel flourished, and it was soon totally refurbished.

During this time I entertained myself by listening to the radio in my Father's office behind the reception area, so I did not feel isolated, particularly as my Father and whoever was on reception duties at the time were always popping in and out. I listened to all the schools programmes, and to Jimmy Young in the mornings, and after lunch Ethel joined me in our flat, and we had the TV on.

I could always tell when Ethel used to drop off to sleep. I know when my Father, or anyone, has gone to sleep in their chair as their breathing changes. Few things escape me – I can tell a lot even from footsteps.

Every night Mother and Father worked until quite late, and would then have dinner in the restaurant at about 9.30 p.m. But I was not lonely. The reception staff and hall porters used to sneak into my room to watch television with me, particularly when *Dallas* was on! One reception-ist called Maxine and I talked about the Ewing family a lot. Michael, a porter loved *Mash* – so I enjoyed it as well.

You know – I couldn't have done without them. They were so good to me, and I am grateful to them. I have always tried to make friends with the staff of not only the Grange, but also other hotels I have visited – my friend-ships are long-lasting.

As you will have gathered, both my parents were extremely busy, and even fitting in my bathtime was often difficult. I never resented their absence, and although I know my Mother still feels guilty because she felt she was neglecting me at this time, but I understand that it was all for the right reasons, to give me a secure financial future. I certainly did not waste any of my time. I took in, and still do, everything I heard and used the time to educate myself with the help of the TV and radio, and this has made me quite an expert on quiz programmes, because of my reten-tive memory. One of my main reasons for liking them is because I usually answer all the questions!

As I have said, there are a lot of things I cannot do; I cannot cope with stress, and sometimes I struggle with my moods and emotions. But my mind retains facts like a sponge soaking up water. For example to illustrate this point, in an edition of *University Challenge* which was on

TV when I was writing this book, Liverpool scored 105, Robinson College, Cambridge, scored 255, and I scored 230. I missed a few because they were picture questions!

Because of my love of music, I appear to have gained a reputation in this field, again due to my memory. For example, Tony Loose, who claims to be the oldest disc jockey in the country, used to ask me questions rather than ring the BBC music library! He has a dance studio at Lymington, and we still keep in touch.

Around this time my parents asked a local typing teacher, Janet Thorpe, to try to teach me to touch-type. Because of the stiffness in my hands, and my difficulty in following a straight line, it proved to be quite a task. Mother stuck a piece of Elastoplast on the centre keys and I persevered. To encourage me, the village policeman asked me to type a short story he had written. It took six months, but I did it, with Janet's invaluable help. I also helped a little in reception, by typing booking confirmations, with supervision!

12

During 1972 there was a bit of excitement, when my parents considered buying an hotel in Jersey. They liked the island and looked seriously at several hotels. They made an offer for one called Waters Edge. Their offer was accepted, and my Father in particular was very thrilled. They found out that Bob Monkhouse had spent time there, and promised to come and stay if my parents bought the hotel, but after about 18 months of negotiation the deal fell through. I was pleased because I wanted to stay at the Bramley Grange.

Other events of the early/middle seventies which stand out in my memory include the Guildford floods of 1973, when the whole town was nearly submerged. It was the week of the Farnborough airshow, so the hotel was already full. Many travellers were stranded, and there were local people whose homes were literally in feet of water. Many were relieved to have some shelter, and over 50 people slept on the floor of the residents' lounge.

In 1974 a film company asked if they could use the grounds of the hotel for the background of a film called *Young Mozart*. Mother and Father readily agreed, and when the film was completed, they were invited to Vienna for the premiere. Unfortunately, they could not spare the time to go.

All this time my parents continued to maintain the good reputation of the hotel and the Halloween of 1974 was very memorable. It was a charity night for the Cheshire Homes and Mother spent hours decorating the hotel and putting candles everywhere, including in the garden. My Father made spider's webs and changed every light bulb to a different colour. All the staff were dressed up as witches. Everyone said it looked just like a cave! A number of model witches were made, and one was hoisted above the reception area. My father kept shouting, 'Pam, come down from there!' It was great fun.

The Bramley Grange was very much a focal point of the village, and we all got involved in a lot of things. For example, I used to go singing at a local retirement home. It was very enjoyable, and I became friendly with the choirmaster. Once when I sang folk songs, hymns and songs from the shows along with the others, I put so much effort into it that I think I strained myself and went hoarse.

One morning shortly after, I was coughing and coughing, and I brought up over half a pint of blood. Father was very worried and called out Ian, our doctor. He came immediately although it was only seven o'clock in the morning. He arranged for me to go to hospital, where they fed an optical fibre camera into my stomach. The doctor said he had never seen so many polyps, but let them be, they were doing no harm – and in fact they have caused me no trouble since then. So I had to give up singing, as my strenuous efforts put too much strain on my vocal chords.

I continued my studies because I always believe in keeping up my education. I was still enjoying my music, and still watching television with Ethel, and, if I may confess, we gambled! Ethel had an account with the tote, and we had the occasional small bet. If it sounds strange when I say 'watching TV' when I am blind, I really do get a lot out of it. My favourite programmes are sport, and then quizzes and comedy shows.

My Father and I went to the Bramley Social Club and, best of all, the Jolly Farmer, the village pub. Dubonnet and lemonade was my favourite drink. We went every Thursday and Sunday to play the jukebox. To get into the pub we had to go through the kitchens, as the steps in the front were too steep for my wheelchair. We were also involved in fund-raising and village cricket. A very proud moment was when I opened the new wing of the Bramley Social Club. It may interest you to know they asked me to cut the tape of the new Ruby Lounge, and I made a little speech.

These years were both exciting and happy, and basically life was great – well, unless you count the times I fell out of my wheelchair!

One evening I was on my way to the social club with my Father when my chair hit a bump, and I was catapulted out, falling on my face. Having no sight, I did not think to put my hands out to save myself. My Father got me back into the chair and back to the hotel. Our doctor came round straightaway, and said I must go to hospital immediately. Father phoned a specialist friend of his, a Mr Attenborough, and asked him if he could meet us at the hospital. Late as it was, he readily agreed, and was there when we arrived. Both my Father and I were so grateful.

I had lost a tooth, and had stitches in my mouth, but was allowed to go home – and do you know, my Father never got a bill from Mr Attenborough. He said he could not remember the incident. What a kind man!

Then there was the day when my Mother decided to take me out in her cabriolet car, as she knew I travelled well if the hood was down. She took me out to the car park, and lifted me out of the wheelchair to put me in the front seat, and as she lowered me into the car, my foot got stuck between the seat and the door ledge as she twisted me around – and I went into spasm. Mother could not see what had happened, so lifted me again, and we both fell backwards onto the ground of the car park, me on top of my Mother. Unfortunately the damage had been done, and the subsequent X-ray showed a fracture of the ankle. As the doctor at the hospital explained, the bones of people who have never walked, do not develop and he likened them to lace, so they are very easily injured.

Apart from these mishaps, things ran quite smoothly – that is, until we acquired a new family pet!

Simba, the Old English mastiff, died in the heat of the summer of 1976, so we were left without a pet. Both my parents and I were so upset, and I remember my Father saying he would never have another dog, because it had been awful to have Simba put down when he became so ill. Mother thought differently. She heard from the St Bernard Rescue people that a dog was being held in the unlikely custody of a north London police station. Mother said she could not bear the thought of him being put down, so she asked Ivan, a family friend, if he would collect him. This was on Boxing Day, and Ivan duly arrived back with what he described as a 'complete nutter'. Not to be deterred, we all made this poor animal feel very welcome, and called him Santa.

Mother gave him about 5 pounds of cold beef and 8 pints of milk. He scoffed the lot, and we left him to settle in and find his feet. Unfortunately, he found his feet behind the cold buffet set out in the ballroom. He had pulled a whole turkey off the table, and eaten the lot.

A few weeks later Santa had company. My Father was playing snooker when Mother walked in with a man from the English Mastiff Rescue Service.

'No, absolutely not,' said my Father, knowing what was in my Mother's mind.

'Just one night?' pleaded the man holding the dog.

Needless to say, one night turned into another and another.

This mastiff was called Rocky. He got on very well with Santa, and they both became part of the hotel life. My Father had a few problems training them. One morning he had them on leads when they took off, dragging him up a grass bank on his stomach. A bedroom window opened, and a voice called out, 'Are you all right?'

'Yes, thank you,' replied my Father. 'I'm just training them.'

'You're not doing a very good job, are you? But they are very beautiful.'

'Who?' asked Father.

'All of you.' It was Pat Phoenix, the actress, who was staying at the hotel.

Every year, when the Miss World contest was held, we held our own version, in the hotel bar, with relatives, friends and staff as contestants. Every year we crowned the same winner – Ethel. As you will remember, my friend Ethel was small, rather tubby and in her middle sixties, but to me she was the most beautiful person in the world, so she always won. My Mother always entered under the name of Miss Gorgonzola, and one year sent herself 250,000 postal votes – but I still made sure that Ethel won. The hotel guests fell in with our little ceremony, and joined in the celebrations.

A Gurkha reunion was planned to take place at the Bramley Grange, and Princess Anne was due to be present. A police inspector from the Home Office came to give the hotel an inspection, as it was suggested that the Princess might stay the night. Evidently everything was all right, but at the last moment the reunion was switched to a large house and estate nearby because it could cater for 800 people, and we could cater for only 200. My Mother and Father were invited to the occasion, which included about 14 guests to sit down and dine with Princess Anne. My Mother sat next to the artist David Shepherd, and my Father sat next to President Eisenhower's granddaughter. They had a wonderful evening, but the point of my story is that if my Father met the Princess he must tell her how unlucky I thought she was at the Badminton Horse Trials that year. He did meet her, and gave her my message. The Princess said, 'Thank your daughter very much, and tell her that I was very fortunate to get as far as I did!'

For many years we used to invite elderly patients from St George's Hospital in London to come down in a coach for lunch and tea. They all enjoyed it very much, and I got to know many of them. One wrote to my parents to the effect that she had never thought she would see heaven before she died. She lived in the East End of London, and her only toilet was at the bottom of the garden.

There was a time at the hotel which was very interesting indeed. It was when the Harrier aircraft was being tested at nearby Dunsfold aerodrome. There were a number of countries involved in trying out the aircraft and all the representatives of these countries stayed at the hotel. There were test pilots from America, Sweden, Peru, Egypt and Kenya staying for several weeks. We got to know them very well, and often had dinner with them at night.

Also staying at the same time were about 36 senior policemen who were involved in some internal investigation. They stayed for just on a year. The pilots and the police got on well together and enjoyed each other's company on the squash court, snooker table, putting green, and going jogging around the golf course at 7 a.m. in the mornings — led by my parents!

It was a very enjoyable time, and my Father presented one of his cricket bats to the Americans when they left.

13

Because the hotel was going so well, my parents decided to expand the business further. My Father had bought the freehold of the hotel and grounds in the early 1970s and now borrowed again from the bank and built 16 luxury one-bedroomed service flats. Each had a kitchen, bathroom and living room overlooking the gardens. I think the initial plan was to sell to businessmen working in the South-East or young career couples who would want to combine country living with all the advantages of the hotel and its facilities, which at the time even included a squash court. As it turned out, the flats were snapped up by elderly people who saw a lot to be gained from living in a hotel complex, never short of company, an excellent restaurant on hand, no building or maintenance worries, and it was all very secure.

My Father was pleased with the building work and set about the final preparations to sell the flats. This was to be the beginning of a very worrying time for him and my Mother. They had asked for planning permission to build and sell the flats on a long lease. The application was refused and my Father was told that the planning officers had put the wrong category on the planning form and that he would have to re-apply. On 22 September 1978 the *Surrey Advertiser* first reported our dilemma. My Father was quite open about the financial problems. The planning committee refused to budge, saying it was believed the flats were hotel accommodation. The planning officers kept repeating over 14 meetings that it was their mistake and that my Father was the one suffering for it.

The disagreement went on for over two years. Mother and Father talked about it nearly all the time, it worried them so much. The local paper continued to report on it. My Father was even on national TV – ITV to be exact – just after the News at Six. A television crew came down and filmed the hotel and interviewed my Father. Not wishing to rock the boat too much, he played it down as much as possible, and said that there had obviously been a misunderstanding between the planning officers and the committee and he hoped they would soon sort it out as he was paying the bank a huge amount of interest charges through no fault of his own.

ITV really went to town, starting their story, 'Bureaucracy gone mad in Surrey'. The local paper continued to report on it; if my Father lost it meant that the hotel would have to be sold. Eventually the Government Ombudsman was called in to investigate. The story was still in the paper every week; in 1979 it appeared as the editorial eight times. The villagers wrote giving their support. Mother read one of the published letters to me and it went as follows:

Sir, I have been attempting to follow the fortunes or rather misfortunes of the Bramley Grange Hotel and its proprietor Mr Ken Taylor over the last few months. I have only a nodding acquaintance with Mr Taylor but I know him to be a man of integrity and some courage. It is therefore with some dismay that I have watched the apparent public humiliation that he has had to undergo at the hands of the Waverley District Council ...

You can imagine what it was like at home. Mother said that Father had aged ten years with the stress. By August 1979 it was clear that we had won but the *Surrey Advertiser* continued to print reports of the enquiry and to tell how much my Father had spent on interest payments. He very nearly lost everything and in December 1979 the paper announced that Mr William Whitelaw (now Lord Whitelaw) the Home Secretary at the time, 'had been asked to probe the running of Local Government'. Fortunately, there was a happy ending and a 99-year lease was granted. The flats were sold and we all breathed a big sigh of relief.

My Mother always says that every cloud has a silver lining and she believes that someone up there is always looking after us.

Whilst we had the problems with the flats, we were at least allowed to let them as hotel accommodation, and during this time the Brighton football team stayed. Brian Clough and Peter Taylor were then in charge, and Jimmy Case and Steve Foster were playing for them. For a bit of fun my Mother asked all the team to sign a menu, and when they had kindly done so, she wrote across the top 'We the undersigned agree that this was the best meal we have ever had', and gave it to the chef. It caused a great deal of amusement.

On another occasion the Nottinghamshire county cricket team stayed at the hotel. At that time Jacky Bond was captain and manager, and that great West Indies cricketer Garry Sobers (subsequently Sir Garfield Sobers) was in the side. Whilst my Father and I were having a drink in the bar, most of the players came in, and we were introduced to them. My Father said to Garry Sobers that Peter West, the commentator, had referred to him as the greatest all-rounder ever. Mr Sobers replied that was very kind of Mr West.

'But what did you say, Gail?' my Father asked.

'I'm afraid I said "rubbish".'

'And why was that?' asked Mr Sobers.

'Because I think my Father was the greatest all-rounder, ever.'

'I think you are probably right, Gail. May I be the second greatest?'

And we left it at that.

My Father played Garry at squash (as we had our own court then), and also took both Garry and Jacky Bond to play golf with him at the nearby Bramley course. He said later that they were both excellent golfers, and he enjoyed their company immensely.

When we heard that Mr Sobers had been knighted, I asked my Father whether I could send him a congratulatory telegram. It read: 'To the second greatest all-rounder in the world. Congratulations on your richly deserved knighthood. All my love Gail.' When my Father phoned this message through, the telephone operator asked who is the greatest all-rounder then? My Father jokingly replied, 'I am.'

'Who are you?'

'I'm Gail's Father.'

'Oh, fair enough.'

We all enjoyed and shared in this incident.

14

In the early 1980s I was introduced to the world of ball-room dancing. Bobby and Linda Short and Len Crane (Linda's Father) organise most of the professional and amateur dancing competitions in Great Britain. They like to arrange social 'get-togethers' for those people who are connected to the world of dance, and consequently they booked several dinner/dance events at the hotel.

At the first of these events, my Father and I were having a drink together when Bill Irvine, OBE, a leading figure and judge in dancing, asked if we would like to join them and listen to the music. I was very thrilled and met many of the dancers and their guests.

Bobby and Linda immediately included me in their cir-cle, and we have since become very good friends, and have shared weekends and Christmases away together at various hotels around the country.

At the United Kingdom Championships at the Bourne-mouth International Centre I listen intently to all the con-versation going on around me and can often pick a winner. In my opinion Angela Rippon was the best compère. We were fortunate in being let into rehearsals – I have to say there is the occasional advantage to being disabled, it brings the odd privilege! I have met so many people through dancing and feel very lucky.

Dance News used to entertain some Japanese dancers at Bramley Grange before they went to London and many of them became good friends. There was one called Johnny, a sort of Frank Sinatra of Tokyo. He wheeled me into the middle of the floor and serenaded me. Getting down on one knee, he sang, '*I Can't Help Falling in Love With You*'. The year after, he came back again and asked to see me. I felt really flattered that he had remembered my name.

At one of the *Dance News* functions just before Christmas at the hotel, there was always a cabaret and on one occasion they asked me to sing! I sang *As Time Goes By* – and everyone was very kind and applauded.

Our family became well known on the dance circuit and a whole new world opened up. At one event in Southampton Bobby and Linda asked my Father if he would sponsor a couple from Norway. He agreed and did it in my name so I was included on the programme. They won! They gave me a Norwegian flag and invited us all to the Mayor's reception afterwards.

It began my interest in dancing competitions. I loved every minute of the music and the atmosphere, and I never refused an opportunity to attend, if it was possible.

On one of these occasions, when we were invited to the United Kingdom Dance Championships at Bournemouth (which was televised and shown on the BBC), I met a band leader whose name was Tony Evans. He was staying in the same hotel, and kindly gave me some of his cassettes of recordings made by his orchestra. He also invited me to their afternoon rehearsal.

Unfortunately, after lunch whilst my Father was pushing me back to our room in the hotel, my wheelchair hit a small step and I was thrown out, hitting the floor with my face. (I should explain here that when something unusual or unexpected happens, as in this case, I go into spasm. My body stiffens up, and I am incapable of protecting myself.)

The result of my fall was that my nose was split open, and there was blood everywhere. My parents were frantic. My Father managed to gather me up and put me back into my wheelchair with the help of the restaurant manager, and eventually got me into the car. My Mother sat with me and gathered some towels together to catch the blood. By now I was in a panic. My Mother was trying to calm me, saying, 'Take deep breaths through your mouth.' This I did, but I was still very frightened.

Once we were inside the casualty department of Poole hospital, a young lady doctor took charge, and whilst she inserted seven stitches my Father held me and told me that the stitches were blue – my favourite colour. I did not realise at the time, but as soon as the doctor had taken over, my Mother was reduced to crying outside.

The doctor did a great job on my nose, but I was told later I looked a bit of a mess, with swollen lips, two black eyes and a patchwork nose. No wonder my Mother was so upset, and left poor Father to cope.

After all this, I still wanted to go to the competition, but I was overruled and went to bed instead, and we drove home the next morning.

By the way, Tony Evans invited us to his home for dinner and even made a recording with his band, a version of '*Mack the Knife*', calling it '*Gail the Knife*'.

We continued to enjoy weekends away, and some of the most enjoyable were the annual reunions of my Father's old schoolfriends, normally held at Sidmouth in Devon. About 20 or 30 stay at the same hotel, and we have a wonderful time. Two very special people used to come away with us. They were Father's cousin Graham Wylie and his wife Joan. In fact Graham was born next door to my Father. They have always been very close to me, and often come to stay the weekend.

We were still very much involved in village life, and my

parents helped to raise funds for a new sports pavilion for the cricket and football club. It took about a year but was built in the end. Tony Hart, the artist and TV presenter, opened it. When I think back to my early days – a cabbage – *huh*! How things had changed.

15

Soon after I was able to talk, when Tina, our St Bernard, was still around, my Father decided to introduce me to religion in greater detail. He took me down to the local church, between services, on one of our outings with Tina. My Father tied her to a heavy oak seat in the grounds, and we went into the church. It was Harvest Festival time, and the church was full of harvest offerings. The mixed scent of the fruit, the bread, and the flowers, I can still remember.

My Father explained to me that Jesus was my best friend, but I replied, 'No, Jennifer is.' He decided that the best course of action, at that stage, was to adopt my suggestion, and agreed that I now had two 'best friends' – Jennifer and Jesus. He talked to me in general terms about the meaning of the Christian faith, but my first detailed introduction to religion was interrupted by a scratching noise at the church door. Surprise! Surprise! Tina had managed to pull the oak seat across the lawn outside the church, obviously wanting to join in our religious discussions!

I would like to talk a little about my faith. By and large I feel that this is a very personal and private matter, and each person has to find their own way of dealing with life and all its difficulties. The comedian Dave Allen used to say

'May your God go with you', and I think that this is a wise way to look at things. At the end of the day, wherever we are in the world, I believe that we are praying to one and the same 'Being'. Like my parents I believe that God is taking care of each one of us. You could say that I, along with many other disabled people, have reason to feel frustrated, angry, trapped and quite desperate at times. I cannot go for a good walk or get in the car and drive away, because I am totally dependent on other people to meet every one of my physical needs. Over the years I hope that I have coped well, but, if I am honest, there have been moments when, like everyone, I have felt depressed, and it is in the bleak times that God really does comfort me. I am never going to walk or see, although my parents have tried every option in both conventional and complementary medicine.

For example, I received treatment from a Mr Selmes, who lived in the nearby village of Chilworth. He had treated members of the Royal Family, and was well respected internationally. Whilst he had treated his patients in London, on reaching the age of 90, and as driving his Morris Minor became more difficult, many patients came to him and received treatment whilst staying at the Bramley Grange. Mr Selmes kindly offered his expertise to me, free of charge, as he hoped to improve my physical condition. He even 'studied' popular music so that he could converse with me on a subject I was interested in! Unfortunately, despite his best efforts, his treatment did not improve my condition. But Mr Selmes taught me about more important things, and I am most grateful to have met such a remarkable man. I like to think that I accept my situation with grace and am happy. There is nothing to be gained by being bitter. My strong faith helps to sustain me, and I talk to God as a friend.

As I continued with my academic studies, I decided to

give some thought to my religious life. The Reverend Tom Farrell, the vicar at the parish church in Wonersh, a neighbouring village, came for a chat and agreed to take me for confirmation classes. He was a very nice man and was captain of the athletics team in the 1969 Rome Olympics. Unlike many vicars, he did not talk down to me or treat me in a condescending way. He respected what I thought – for instance, I really do think that God created the world. I feel very close to Him and that is one reason why I listen to all the religious programmes, like the BBC's '*Songs of Praise*', and particularly look forward to the Remembrance Day Service at the Cenotaph in London. This is also very important and I think we should remember what happened in the wars.

In my confirmation classes it soon became obvious that I knew as much of the Bible as Tom because I had absorbed so much over the years and I already knew the Creed from the radio. I love all the hymns and to choose favourites for my confirmation was difficult. I am fond of *Morning has broken*, *At the name of Jesus*, and *He who should valiant be*, but *Abide with me* is extra special. I can really identify with some of the words. 'When other helpers fail, and comforts flee, help of the helpless, O abide with me.'

The exact date of my confirmation was 20 May 1984. It was a beautiful service. Amongst the people who were there, was my godfather, Sir Geraint Evans and Lady Evans, and the American artist Phil Bailey, lead singer with the pop group Earth, Wind and Fire. Phil was staying in the hotel while cutting an album with Phil Collins and Eric Clapton. We became very good friends and he kindly offered to sing a beautiful gospel song in church called *Safe in God's love*. I would say that Phil is very spiritual and I am pleased to have known him.

My friend Ann Bradley remembers the day clearly

because it seemed almost bizarre to see Phil singing in the local church alongside Geraint and to have all those people supporting me. When Philip finished his solo there was absolute silence for a moment. I clapped. It seemed the only thing to do to show how much I appreciated what he had done.

My Father had teased the vicar when we arrived. The vicar asked him what would Phil be singing. '*Rock Around the Clock* and *Jailhouse Blues*,' my Father told him.

'Oh no,' exclaimed the vicar.

'Just joking,' said my Father.

My Mother had invited all the people at the church to come back to the hotel for a buffet and drinks, and about 80 came back with us.

The Bishop of Dorking, Kenneth Evans, performed the ceremony and he came back to the hotel with Geraint and Brenda, Phil Bailey, Graham and Joan Wylie and quite a few others. We sat down to dinner about 20 in all. I remember the Bishop saying, 'I may be only a bishop, but tonight I have been treated like a king!' It was without doubt one of the best days of my life, and Brenda said recently, 'Gail's confirmation was a very moving occasion!'

God is always there for me and that thought brings such a lot of comfort because my parents are getting older and I don't know what the future holds. I just trust that I will be kept safe and that His love will never fail me. I really believe that, although I know that Mother and Father have lots of ideas for my being looked after, if anything happens to them.

Any parent with a handicapped child must worry about the future irrespective of how much money is available. As Mother says, no one can live without love, and the difficult question is how to provide long-term genuine loving care. She and Father had decided to keep a large portion of land, known as the paddock, when the hotel was sold. Their ambition is to build flats for disabled people and their families so that when carers died, someone like me could either continue in the same apartment with assistance or live in a nursing wing within a familiar stable environment. Mother continues to try to get insurance companies to support the scheme in cases where large amounts of compensation were paid. She would love to see this dream come true, to build a home where everyone helps in whatever small way, either on the switchboard, or in the kitchen. Well, Mother, you and Father were the ones who taught me about dreams coming true!

In the meantime, they are making plans to ask a nursing service to come in once or twice a month so that they get to know and understand my needs. You see, it isn't the niceties of life which are going to matter – I know my friends will still come and see me. There's a lot more to looking after me, like taking me to the loo, keeping an eye on any pressure sores and things like that. Mother makes sure my food is good; I'd be devastated if I got an upset tummy, for obvious reasons. Help is needed to blow my nose; this is the reality of life.

I would like to end this chapter by saying quite simply that I believe God will sustain me no matter what my problems are.

16

Between 1981 and 1985 life was pleasant and settled. Each day I still went down to the kitchen to help a lady called Mrs Faulkner with the washing-up. She was a very jolly person and I must tell you I particularly enjoyed her company. She laughed and joked as we listened to the radio. For years our favourite programme used to be *Music While You Work* – we loved singing along. Then I had lunch with Ethel, followed by an afternoon in front of the television. The commercials made me laugh! The best one was for PG Tips tea when one of the monkeys said, 'Do you know the piano's on my foot?' and the other one replied, 'You hum it, son, and I'll play it!' On a more serious note, I carried on with my studies in French and German. My parents were so busy with the hotel we were not able to have holidays, but occasionally we went for a day to the coast, usually a town in West Sussex like East Preston or Rustington.

Mother was still doing a lot of the hotel cooking, running the reception and, frankly, not getting any younger. And so my Father wondered if it was time to consider moving on. As I have admitted to you, unfortunately I am not very good at accepting changes, and when my Father said he was thinking of selling the hotel I was very upset. For about three days I was dreadful to live with. I thought I would lose all my friends and the staff I was so fond of, and adapting to a new home would not have been easy. I really did not want to move to Jersey or anywhere else. We live in a lovely large apartment which extends over the hotel reception and into the new block of flats. A balcony looked over the gardens and my room had a door opening directly to the balcony outside. My Father had said I would always have a base to come back to because the property had been transferred into my name. Friends popped in all the time and I was never lonely.

In March 1986, the hotel was sold. As it turned out, to my relief, we stayed. However, Father was still keen to stay in the hotel trade, perhaps financing a small establishment as a silent partner. He and Mother looked at a hotel on the island of Sark. I know Mother was hoping we might move over to the Channel Islands and she thought a close-knit community would be good for me. But my Father was very concerned at even getting me over there, on and off a plane and a boat. As you will no doubt remember, I find travelling a bit unnerving because of not having any sense of motion. I feel muddled and disorientated and, to be honest, although I know I'm being looked after, it is hard for me. So, even though there was a tremendous appeal to my parents that we had a second home on Sark, plus a stake in a business, not to mention the tax advantages, they decided to stay put in Bramley, lock, stock, barrel and yours truly.

Frankly, I had not realised how much I had missed my Mother, whilst she had been busy helping run the hotel and now she has more time we are able to do a lot more things together. It was time for everyone to relax, and we went away for Christmas to the Goodwood Park Hotel near Chichester. Our dancing friends Linda and Bobby came with us. On Boxing Day our St Bernard dog pulled me into the function room dressed as a reindeer – the dog, that is, not me. We had a lot of fun! I felt very happy.

Back home, we played music in my 'den', went out to lunch at the coast, or to the Forte Crest Hotel near Guildford. I am well known and well received there and access is easy for my wheelchair, so this was and still is one of the best outings. They have music groups playing during Sunday lunch.

Music, as you know, is desperately important to me and I am fortunate in being able to ring a local shop in Godalming and have anything I want ordered, usually something I have heard and liked on the radio. The owner at Record Corner, Tom Briggs, always recognises my voice and says in a very friendly way which flatters me, 'Hello, luv, how are you?' I order a lot of easy-listening cassette tapes. It's difficult for me to be pushed around the town, and being lifted in and out of the car is again difficult although we have tried all the aids on the market, I'm conscious of the hard work involved in pushing me around – it's a nightmare in a supermarket and it upsets me if I feel I'm being a nuisance.

Mother and I go shopping occasionally, but I have to say that I am not all that interested in clothes. Perhaps I should expand on what it is like to be blind and not know what you look like. Mostly I wear trousers, slippers and a good sweater, so I am smart and comfortable. The slippers are because I have no ankles to speak of; you see, when you can't walk the calf muscles never develop.

For special events Mother bought me three Gina Frattini gowns; a black velvet one makes me feel particularly good. I like a shop in Cranleigh called Asparagus, where they are extremely helpful. I have some Mondi and Yarrell jumpers and I love Escada perfume; after that I would choose Christian Dior perfume.

It may interest you to know why my favourite colour is blue. This is because I have been told that the sea and the sky are blue, so this colour, in my opinion must be beautiful. I only know about nature from the smells. For example, the freshness of the rain, and the fragrance of flowers.

I can usually tell what my Mother is preparing, food wise. Each type of meat has a different aroma, as do vegetables, salad or fruit. I never have to ask what is being cooked, as I clearly recognise the various ingredients from their smell.

As I have explained already, my other senses more than compensate for my lack of sight, and the only thing I miss is the expressions on people's faces. Consequently it is not always easy for me to realise someone is 'leg-pulling', or to appreciate visual humour.

Physical contact is so very important to me, and I do appreciate the holding or touching of hands. Also the frequent use of my name in general or specific conversation is nice – but then I think these things apply to everyone.

I have said that music can snap me out of any mood but I would also like to say that a warm, sincere voice is like having a friend with me all the time. I hope she will not mind if I say it, but Sarah Kennedy is excellent and she makes a good start to my day. She makes me feel happy. She's cheerful, funny, and if she thinks something is wrong she doesn't pull her punches. She's not flippant but she gets her point across.

One of my hobbies is making tapes, in the same way as a DJ would record a radio programme. I record these under the name of 'Gail Cleverclogs', since the manager of the hotel gave me this nickname after trying to catch me out with a number of trick questions on music, without success.

As an ardent fan of Ronnie Hilton's programme, *Sounds of the Fifties*, I used to record all his programmes. I wrote to him to tell him how much I enjoyed them, and sent him a copy of one of my tapes. He was very kind and mentioned me twice on Radio 2, quoting me as Gail Cleverclogs of Guildford. He congratulated me on my tape:

RONNIE HILTON

14th September, 1992.

Dear Gail,

Very many thanks for the tapes you sent, for all the time and trouble you went to for us. Thanks for your birthday wishes too. We had a lovely meal that night at a Cantonese/Peking restaurant with our son Simon, his lady, Tina and us. Simon is an instructor at the Brands Hatch Racing School and races whenever he can raise the sponsorship.

The Bing tapes are excellent and such fun. Fabulous arrangements. Aren't they the records/numbers where they lifted Bing's voice and put them on to newer arrangements and backings? When you next write maybe you'd let us know the title, label and number of the albums so we can ask Pete Johnson to "pull" them from the library.

Forgive the short letter but after a week away – the journey to Rhyl was a nightmare, took nine hours and we arrived fifteen minutes after the show had started total nervous wrecks – I'm now trying to do about a dozen jobs at once to catch up.

Thanks again Gail from us both, the tapes kept us sane during the journeys last week.

Love to your Mother and of course, to you from us both,

Ronnie &   Chrissie
xx

My Father considers my DJ tapes to be very good indeed. In fact, he goes as far as to say that he thinks they are as good as any professional DJ. I try to give a lot of information about the music, between the various tracks.

It may also interest you to know how important a good commentator is to blind people. I will explain. You see, he or she must tell you what is going on, every detail of it, without driving those who have sight completely round the bend. Some of the best are Bill MacLaren on rugby, Peter Alliss on golf, and Ted Lowe on snooker. Mind you, the late Brian Johnston was the best. He went into every detail there was. I have to listen intently to sport, and thanks to these fine commentators I get a lot out of it.

It is a pity that none of my favourite sports commentators were present at a sporting achievement by my Father in February 1995. Whilst playing golf at his local club, he managed to get a hole in one at the fourth hole. There was much jubilation from his partners and they carried on playing their round. When they reached the sixteenth tee, which is by the clubhouse, my Father popped in to tell the Secretary and ask the bar to set up a 'slate' for everybody to have a drink on him. He told them that he would not be able to get back himself as he had to get home to assist me.

He carried on playing the sixteenth and when driving off the seventeenth hit another very good shot, which appeared to be straight on the flag. When they arrived on the green, they discovered my Father's ball in the hole.

Two holes in one in one round! This was too much for my dear old dad to ignore, so after playing the eighteenth, his friends went into the clubhouse to inform the Secretary again, whilst my Father rushed home to tell my Mother and myself of his exploits. After he had seen to my needs, my Mother insisted he went back to the golf club to join in the celebrations, which suggestion my Father was only too pleased to take.

I think that it cost him rather a large amount of money, but he had a really wonderful time.

The golf club informed all the relevant organisations, including the *Guinness Book of Records*, and the next morning, my Father received numerous telephone calls from national newspapers and golf magazines, asking for details and photographs, and even a call from BBC South, who wanted him to go to the studio and speak about the event.

Talk about everyone having 15 minutes of fame during their lifetime – this was my Father's 15 minutes. He really lapped it up and, I am told, is still milking it at the golf club, who very kindly presented him with a special tie and a glass ornament with a special inscription on it.

It was all very exciting for a while. I remember a part of the interview on the radio, which I taped. The interviewer asked my Father how he had accomplished such a feat and my Father replied, 'Luck.' 'No, it can't be luck,' said the interviewer, 'I have been playing golf for forty years and have never done a hole in one.' 'Look,' said my Father, 'I believe Jack Nicklaus and Nick Faldo have got the edge on me and I don't think they have ever done two holes in one in one round, so it has to be luck.' As I say, my Father lapped it up!

You may be amused, but in my opinion one of the best actors is Peter Falk in *Colombo*. He says things like 'Excuse me' or 'By the way'. I don't have to assume or guess with him, whereas with the benefit of sight you can see from facial expressions or the direction of a gaze what is going on.

Martin Bell gets my vote for news, and for cookery it has to be Delia Smith. She explains everything and is brilliantly descriptive, saying things like, 'I've got some eggs here in my bowl.' It makes me feel as though I am in the kitchen with her, smelling and tasting the food. She has a bubbly personality and a nice sense of humour. I must also mention that David Attenborough scores highly on my list. In his wildlife programmes I can see in my mind the scene he describes. He brings nature to life.

17

I am sure by now you can understand what my life has been like and how lucky I have been in having so many people who love and care for me. Friends are important to all of us but for me they are quite literally my lifeline. I consider it a privilege to know such special people. But apart from those I see on a regular basis I have also been fortunate enough to spend time with a number of celebrities, particularly those who have stayed at the Bramley Grange Hotel. I would like to say how grateful I feel because they seem to offer their friendship to me so easily.

If you remember from earlier chapters, my parents sold the house in Beckenham to Geraint and Brenda Evans. Our families met at least every other week. He was still struggling to make a name at that time and Geraint was away a lot on operatic engagements, but I shall never forget the first time we met. I know that Brenda, (Lady Evans), will bear this out as well. Although she says Geraint was always good with children, there was something special, a bond between us that just clicked – you know, that feeling that you already know someone. Apparently my face used to light up just at the sound of his rich Welsh voice. He used to sing to me. Can you imagine it? A world-famous opera star singing just to me! In those earlier days I couldn't speak, but Geraint knew I liked

Mammy's little baby loves shortnin' bread. It was a catchy tune, and I could listen for hours. A deep affection developed, partly due to my love of music. I know he thought a lot of me and over the years always kept in touch, telling me of the funny things that happened to him on stage, and I always listened to him on the radio. His most famous role was in Verdi's *Falstaff*, and it may interest you to know I have a tape of him being interviewed by Terry Wogan. He taught Terry to sing some chords! I also have videos of his master classes, which are just brilliant. Geraint explained how to create moods like anger or sadness, and would often shout, 'Hold it, hold it,' when they got it wrong. He was so passionate about what he did, but with a wonderful sense of humour. He told me about his meeting in Switzerland with Charlie Chaplin, who was so interested in how he started that it made Geraint feel quite humble.

Everyone was excited when Geraint was invited to lunch at Buckingham Palace. I was particularly thrilled to hear that he had been seated next to Her Majesty Queen Elizabeth, and that much of the conversation had centred around my achievements. A man of great humility, he also confessed to being relieved not to have to talk about himself, and that the first course was not soup; always tricky if you are nervous! Apparently the Queen was interested to hear how I had been educated.

In 1984 Geraint published his autobiography, *A Knight at the Opera*, and I have a copy which he signed 'To my dear Gail, all my love, Geraint'. I was thrilled to be mentioned on page 90. This is what he says: 'Gail is our Godchild. She is a very remarkable young lady, a wonderfully happy person in spite of being spastic and blind... She has a wonderful ear for music. Often she will telephone me to talk about some television programme I have been involved in and I get very emotional when I hear her discussing the programme as if she had actually seen it.'

This is Your Life did a programme on Geraint, and Brenda asked them if it would be possible to record it at the Bramley Grange, so that I could appear, and it would be a complete surprise to Geraint because Brenda would say, 'Let's go down and see Gail'. Unfortunately the producers etc., did not take kindly to the idea, and I was not asked to appear. Geraint was very upset, and after the show he was talking to one of the guests about this, his friend Joseph Cooper, the concert pianist and presenter of the BBC TV programme *Face the Music* who lives only a few miles away from us. Geraint suggested that Joseph should go to see me – 'She watches all your programmes and her knowledge of music is wonderful. Gail always correctly guesses the music you play on your dummy keyboard.'

Joseph Cooper promised that he would visit, and he was as good as his word. So I gained another friend through Geraint, and we still keep in touch, although Joseph has not been in very good health of late, and his lovely wife Carol died recently.

One of Geraint's last appearances was on Sir Harry Secombe's show *Highway* in Aberaeron when they sang a duet. It was great. They both put so much into it. Sir Harry and his wife Myra used to come to the hotel for Sunday lunch and I always looked forward to that. Sir Harry made a fuss of me. One day I said to Myra that when he sang *If I Ruled The World* I wished he did. It would be a better place.

On 21 September 1992, Geraint died. It was terrible news to me, because although I did not see him that often, we were very close. They held a memorial service for him at Westminster Abbey. My Father was to attend but, unfortunately, it was on the morning I twisted my back in bed, and as I had to go to hospital in an ambulance he could not go. I am told that it was a wonderful service, one befitting such a nice man.

I like to talk to singers because of the music, but other people who stand out over the years include the late Joyce Grenfell. I had lunch with her every day for six weeks and we had some wonderful chats. Joyce was a very special lady, kind and so interesting to talk to. After about two weeks, Joyce asked my Father whether I was blind.

'Yes,' replied my Father.

'Not completely blind?' asked Joyce.

'Yes, completely,' said my Father.

'Oh, how stupid of me,' said Joyce, 'I have been having lunch with her all this time and didn't realise she was blind. I just thought she had bad eyesight. But her favourite colour is blue.'

'Yes,' said my Father, 'blue sky, blue sea, she thinks they all sound beautiful. I tell Gail that we see with our eyes and that she sees with her mind and I think that she sees more with her mind that we do with our eyes.'

One morning in December 1983, a young New Zealander enquired at the hotel whether there was any part-time work available, as his main interest was riding and working with horses which took up a considerable amount of his time, and he had not long arrived in this country. He appeared very suitable and responsible, and my parents offered him bar work. He proved to be a great find, and did an excellent job in the bar, being very popular with everyone.

After working with us a few months he asked if he could have some time off to go and be kitted out for the New Zealand Horse Eventing Team, which was to compete in the Los Angeles Olympics. Having duly competed, on his return he brought me back a T-shirt with 'Spirit of the Games' printed upon it.

We had no idea that he was such an excellent rider, as he

had never mentioned his achievements. We were all absolutely thrilled for him, and watch him whenever there are any horse trials on the television – his name is Andrew Nicolson.

Alan Bates stayed at the hotel whilst appearing at the Yvonne Arnaud theatre, and one day I happened to be at the reception desk when he kindly tried to engage me in conversation. Unfortunately, as he did not know my name, I did not realise that he was addressing me – so the poor man got no response. I am sure he was embarrassed and I only wish I could have put the matter right. If we ever meet again I would like to explain as I thought it a very kind gesture on his part.

During Phil Bailey's stay at the hotel, his friend Denise Williams, an American singer with a number two hit in the UK charts called *Let's Hear it for the Boy* came to see him and stayed overnight. Phil told her about me and she kindly asked to meet me. Denise came down to my flat and spent an hour with me talking about music in general. She was very friendly and pleasant to talk to.

Another friend of mine used to visit his Father, who lived in one of the service flats. He was connected to Linda McCartney in her vegetarian foods business and he also happens to live near them. One day he appeared with one of Paul's recordings on cassette with a signed message from him which said 'To Gail, keep rocking, all my love Paul'. This is very special to me as the tape is not on general release – I treasure it.

Nigel Hawthorne was most amusing. At breakfast my Father used to say, 'Good morning, Prime Minister.'

'No, no,' replied Mr Hawthorne, 'just head of the Civil Service.'

He told me once that that night in *Yes, Prime Minister* he would be climbing out on the windowsill to try and get into the Prime Minister's office because the Prime

Minister had locked him out of his office. Again, he had time for me.

So did Patricia Routledge. She even came to see me in the flat a couple of times, and wrote me a lovely letter.

'It's Mrs Bucket, Gail,' said my Father.

'That's Bouquet!' she replied.

I love watching Miss Routledge in *Keeping Up Appearances* because she is just about the funniest person on TV, but I also admire her musical talents and really cherish the time she spent with me.

So you see, my life has been extremely interesting and I can't thank the theatrical people enough for taking an interest in me. They lead busy lives and have many demands on their time but I have encountered nothing but kindness.

Roger and Sue Horton became very close friends in the past few years. Sue is my cousin; we saw quite a bit of them with their sons Chris and Anthony, and Chris often comes to see me. He is very keen on languages and is studying to be a lawyer, and we get on very well together.

I was very fond indeed of Roger, and I know he was very fond of me. So much so, that my Father asked him whether he would be willing to be my guardian if anything happened to my parents, as Geraint, who was my original guardian, had so sadly died. Roger readily agreed and my Mother and Father were truly delighted. Unfortunately, Roger died suddenly on the eve of his fiftieth birthday. I miss him very much.

Some time in 1988 we went to my Mother's Auntie Bett's funeral in Barry in South Wales, and whilst there, we picked up her dog Paddy, a cross between a Labrador and a Welsh collie, and brought him home. He was ten years old. We stayed at the Celtic Manor Hotel in Newport, and whilst we were having dinner, my Mother noticed Stephen Hendry, the snooker player, sitting behind

us, with his manager Ian Doyle. My Father asked them
whether they would be kind enough to have a chat with
me. They readily agreed and I was delighted to meet them
– Stephen gave me a signed photograph of himself. They
were both very nice. I told them that Ted Lowe, the
snooker commentator, had said that people had accused
him of talking too much and he explained that he heard
from a lot of blind 'viewers' who thanked him for explaining what was going on and he would continue to carry on
talking for their sakes. I asked Mr Doyle if he would be
kind enough to thank him for me, and he said he would do
that.

18

On a daily basis I see other people closer to home. One of my best friends currently is Bettine, who lives in one of the ground-floor flats. She has multiple sclerosis and is also in a wheelchair. She gets up to me in the lift and will often stay for a meal and then we do the *Telegraph* crossword together. We share a love of music and generally have a lot to talk about.

Another good friend is Beth Beckers. She used to be landlady of the local pub and she has been coming to see me once or twice a week for many years. We both have a love of music, and she has come away with me for the weekend on a number of occasions. She has a nice family and I am very fond of them all.

A number of years ago a lady called Joy Cottam came to help Mother with the housework, and she has also become a very close friend. She's warm and affectionate, loves music and will sit and listen to tapes with me for hours. She kindly wrote the following poem to me:

Gail, Congratulations on Passing the Exam

I have a wonderful friend called Gail
She's a genius as everyone knows.
She always shows so much kindness
From her head right down to her toes!

Her knowledge is somehow unending,
Ask of her what you may.
I always get the right answer
No matter what time of day.

Although my dear friend cannot see me
She sees me in thought and in mind.
We'll dance and we'll sing together
Until Mother comes up from behind!

What a refreshing break in my day
To join her for coffee or such
And listen to music or chatter away.
I'll always love her so much.

Even though I say it myself, I believe I am good company because I can discuss so many different subjects. Also I am a good listener. I have time for people and am happy to let them talk. I know there is a lot I have not experienced, but with many of life's problems I believe it really is a matter of standing back a little, accepting that there are some things that simply will not change with fretting and fuming, and then taking an honest look at what you can do on a practical level.

So here ends another piece of Gail philosophy on life! You may smile, but believe me, when it comes to difficulties, knowing when to fight and when to go with the flow, I think I can safely say I'm an expert.

Another dear friend of mine is Louise Murphy, whom I met through her Mother, who worked at the hotel for many years. Louise comes to visit me every Sunday morning, and has done so for about 15 years. She invited me to her wedding in June 1995. It was a most beautiful occasion, and Louise looked very lovely.

Another friend of mine is Sid O'Connell from the University of Surrey, with whom I share a love of music.

Sid specialises in computerised music, copying exactly the great composers in style and performance from old music manuscripts, piano rolls and cylinders. It is really quite a work of art, very exacting and time-consuming.

I am very flattered that he brings his final recordings for me to offer my opinion. I really enjoy this and it puts my knowledge of music to the test.

Not long ago he produced, from a lecture he gave to about 200 music students and their lecturers at the university, a piece of music, and asked me if I could identify it – he played eight notes and I said, 'You are playing it on a Technics Digital Piano – the music is *The Golliwog's Cakewalk* by Debussy, and you are playing it backwards.'

'Well done, Gail. Not one of them could identify the piano or the music!'

Two more people who have become good friends of mine are Arthur and Ruth Caiger. Arthur was a probation officer. One night somebody knocked on his front door and when he opened it threw acid in his face, blinding him.

Whilst staying at the hotel, he listened to some music being played in the bar, and liking it, asked the barman what it was.

'It's one of the tapes made by the young lady who lives in the hotel,' Graham, the barman, told him.

'I would like to get in touch with her,' said Arthur – and so another friendship started.

Arthur and his wife, Ruth, come to lunch with me about every two months or so. I wrote the following poem to them both.

Friendship is so wonderful, for the happiness it brings.
Friendship is so wonderful, it makes you want to sing.
Friendship and music seem to go hand in hand
And you meet some lovely people who seem to under-
    stand.

So if music be the food of love, it must play on,
And the company of friends is almost like a song.
So Arthur and Ruth I hold you so very dear to me
And look forward so much to the pleasure of your com-
 pany.

I have a slight curvature of the spine, so my parents
arrange for me to have physio, and every Saturday morning at 8.30 a.m. my physiotherapist arrives. I liken the
treatment to the TV programme *Gladiators* and I say
'Gladiator – ready?' and 'Contender – ready?' and she
really puts me through it!

My first physio was Liz Deacon, who lived in
Godalming with her husband Paul and her two boys
George and Harry. She then became pregnant and gave
birth to a beautiful baby daughter, Anna. Liz used to take
Anna with her on all her visits to patients, so I became a
friend as well as a patient. To my delight Liz asked if I
would like to be Anna's godmother. Liz has now moved to
Jersey with the family, but obviously we keep in touch.

A friend of Liz's, Gaynor Wilson, has taken over as
physio, and although Liz and Gaynor's personalities are
quite different, I enjoy the 'torture', and am delighted
to say that with all this hard work I have improved my
muscles and my movement.

My Mother thought she would set me yet another challenge, and wrote to the University of Surrey enquiring
whether any of their lecturers would be prepared to take
me on to further my German, and to teach me Russian. A
lady phoned and said that she would be pleased to come
and meet me, but if we did not get on, she did not consider
it a worthwhile exercise, and she would not accept the
offer of teaching me. Marina, for this was the lady's name,
arrived for our meeting, and we hit it off immediately.

Marina has taught me for over three years, and I now

speak Russian fluently. She now comes once a fortnight to practise conversational Russian, and a colleague of hers comes alternate weeks to keep up my German, as my contacts with German-speaking people are very limited. I enjoy the company of both these ladies very much.

I would like to tell you a little more about my good friend Ann Bradley and her family. Ann and her husband, Max, owned a florist's shop in Bramley village and soon after we arrived at the Bramley Grange we discovered that Ann was an extremely talented flower-arranger. She used to come to the Grange weekly, and with me alongside, adorned the hotel with many fresh flower arrangements. Ann was brilliant at her craft, and many people derived enormous pleasure from her flower displays.

I became a close friend of Ann and her family, and she has always encouraged and helped me whenever she could. They moved away from Bramley, and bought another shop, and she has now settled at Petworth, in Sussex. She involves herself in local activities, and many charitable events.

Although we do not meet very often nowadays, we are still close friends, and keep in touch regularly. I know that Ann is always there for me, in case of trouble and she kindly wrote the following.

'My friendship with Gail began soon after her parents purchased the Bramley Grange Hotel. As the local florist I was asked to prepare floral arrangements for the many wedding receptions and functions that took place there. The hotel has always been part of my life as my Father who came from London worked at the hotel as 2nd Chef in 1932, and was suddenly taken ill and died, so I grew up in Bramley.

I was very nervous at meeting Gail as I had heard

through local customers who used my shop that Gail was blind, and suffered from cerebral palsy, confined to a wheelchair.

I was not at all prepared for the fantastic person who was to become a dear friend and still is although we have moved to Petworth. The flower arranging was soon moved over to the hotel so Gail could 'help' me.

There seems to be no subject Gail cannot converse about with great knowledge and understanding, especially her great love and interest in music at all these levels is quite amazing.

Gail is also a very caring person and protective of her friends, one never hears her criticise anyone – she always has something complimentary to say. My husband, daughters and their families are also great Gail fans and I share them willingly with Gail.

I must mention Gail's healing powers, which I am sure she does not recognise the importance of – I know of three people that have benefited from her 'touch'. It takes the form of a warmth being transferred through her hands to the area of pain or discomfort which seems to bring immediate relief – I do not want you to run away with the idea that this treatment works every time, but it certainly has done on a number of occasions.

One can only stand back in amazement at her achievements and determination, considering her severe disabilities.

My greatest joy was to be Gail's Guest at her confirmation, when hotel guest Philip Bailey of Earth, Wind and Fire, sang an unaccompanied solo for Gail 'Safe in God's Love' Gail's spontaneous response was 'Well done Phil' – it was magical.

It has always been my wish for Gail and her

achievements to be made public knowledge, either on film or on a television programme as it would provide hope and inspiration to others. Without the loving, undaunted and devoted parents, all this would not have been possible and a great loss to us all.

From your number one fan and dear friend

Ann

Towards the end of 1993 my eyes started running, and I was constantly rubbing them. My doctor diagnosed conjunctivitis and prescribed various eye drops and ointment, but none of them seemed to work. After three or four months my eyes were no better; if anything, they were worse.

My doctor popped in (as he often did to make sure I was all right), and my Mother asked him if I could see an eye specialist, as by this time they were very sore and inflamed. A specialist at the Royal Surrey Hospital in Guildford was suggested, but my Mother had been highly recommended to a Mr Leonard by one of the ladies living in the flats.

Mr Leonard practises in London, and in Ashtead, in Surrey, so we made an appointment to see him at Ashtead Hospital. He is a very caring young man, and a brilliant eye surgeon. He immediately diagnosed ingrowing eyelashes, a condition which he likened to having a toothbrush permanently stuck in your eyes, and said that I must be in great pain. Mr Leonard said that he could operate on them, and take out a small portion of the lower lid, so that they would not shut too tightly.

I do not take bad news too well, and started crying. Mr Leonard said very sensibly that I should go home and think about it. He would operate on one eye at a time as the whole process, under general anaesthetic, would take one and a half hours, was a very delicate exacting operation and I would have to stay in hospital overnight.

I was very upset, and my fear of hospitals got the better of me. However, after I had time to think about it I decided to go ahead, and the appointment was arranged for a Saturday morning at Ashtead.

Before the operation was due to start, my Father asked Mr Leonard if he would consider doing both eyes at the same time. Unfortunately he felt that it would not be possible. After a chat with the anaesthetist they prepared me for the operation. I had every confidence in Mr Leonard.

I was back in my room after three hours, and discovered that Mr Leonard, despite his doubts, had operated on both eyes. And I wasn't even sick after the anaesthetic! My only thought was to go home, but Mr Leonard wanted me to stay for one night, as a three-hour operation is quite stressful. But I was adamant – I could not move in their beds, and I needed my home comforts. Mr Leonard was very sympathetic, and agreed that if my Mother and Father were prepared to take responsibility for me I could go, as no purpose was served by staying in hospital if I was so unhappy. So off home we went, and everything was fine. I awoke Sunday morning, and was ready for a nice roast lunch.

My eyes have been comfortable ever since my operation, and there are no visible scars. Mr Leonard did a marvellous job, and I look forward to meeting him again at some time. He was wonderful to me.

19

About four years ago, unknown to me, my Mother had the bright idea that if I became a Radio Amateur (a ham), I would be able to talk to many people and make plenty of friends wherever we lived, and make use of all the languages I had learnt.

She had not realised how difficult it would be. There are two classes of Radio Amateur and an A and B Licence, two exams of one and a half hours each which include questions on licensing conditions, transmitter interference, operating procedures, and practice and theory.

In addition there is a Morse code exam, in which you have to be able to send and receive Morse at 12 words a minute, to enable you to 'go international'. My Mother was really testing the 'little grey cells', but as mentioned, she had been unaware of the challenge she was setting me.

Being my Mother, with her usual determination, she contacted the Guildford Technical College about the RA course – which of course I could not attend. So she then began canvassing RA members in the local area. 'Teach a blind cerebral palsied girl?' 'You must be joking'. 'She will never manage the technical data, certainly not the Morse'. 'She can't even spell or read'. However, my Mother would not give up, and an unexpected angel made an appearance.

My Mother was shopping in Wonersh, just up the road from us, when a friend she had not seen for some time approached her, a Radio Amateur named Bill Douglas, who used the Bramley Grange Hotel and had held his wedding reception there.

'Hello,' said Bill. 'I've heard on the grapevine that Gail is interested in becoming a Radio Amateur. I would be delighted to help her. It would be a great challenge, but I would be pleased to have a go. Nothing ventured, nothing gained. Would every Tuesday morning be convenient?'

Music to my Mother's ears! 'Oh, that would be fine, thank you, Bill.'

Bill started coming in January 1992, and we started with the theory. I found it very hard work, particularly the working out of wavelengths and frequencies. It all seemed double Dutch to me, as I hadn't a clue as to what it was all about. So Bill and Mother decided to record on tape the whole of the RAE Manual. My Mother read the chapters into the recorder, and Bill added a simple explanation and revision at the end of each chapter as it was completed.

In total, there were 12 90-minute tapes, and I set about memorising the book by heart.

Bill went away to New Zealand for three months in the spring of 1992, and whilst he was away both my Mother and my friend Bettine learnt Morse. Bettine mastered Morse in 24 hours, which made my Mother even more determined – she took a week before she could send Morse.

Unfortunately for them both, it is recognised that people who learn to send and not to read Morse find that reading it is far more difficult. However, they helped me a great deal, and by October 1992 with the help of Bill, Bettine and my Mother, I was reading Morse very well and had taught myself spelling – something I had never had to do previously.

I took the Morse exam on 18 October 1992 and gained 100 per cent marks. I was over the moon. I had learnt to read Morse and to spell in ten months, so I studied hard to memorise the tapes and took the remaining RA exams in December 1992.

I failed.

I had wanted to contact Bill, who was again away in New Zealand, but passing the exams was a lot harder than I thought it would be, and for me it was very very difficult to understand. Learning Russian was a piece of cake to this! I am not excusing myself, but unfortunately as I have mentioned, on the day of the Memorial Service for Geraint and just three nights before these exams I tried to turn over in bed and didn't quite make it – my top half went over, and the bottom half stayed put. I did not want to bother my parents by calling out, and by the morning I was in agony. Every time they tried to move me I cried out in pain. My dear kind doctor came, and suggested an X-ray should be taken before he made a diagnosis. An ambulance came and I was taken to Mount Alvernia Hospital. Every moment of the journey, and every bump, was purgatory. The x-ray showed nothing but they said I had torn my back muscles. I remained in constant pain and stayed in bed on painkillers. I was also vomiting and could not eat or drink for a couple of days. My Mother wanted to call off my sitting the exams, but I insisted on taking them as they are only held twice a year, and I did so want to be able to call Bill in New Zealand. It was not to be. I had been in pain for three weeks and I was far too ambitious. After all, the courses for the technical exam take a year and I was too impatient and confident, so I had to learn the hard way. My first failure.

Mother thought it was all too testing and stressful, and felt guilty at setting me such a hard task. 'Gail, I do think you should forget it – you have achieved so much. It is not

102

fair to put you under such stress. Shall we call it a day? I'm sorry, I never realised how difficult it would be.'

'NO! I want to go on and pass my exams. I am not worried about learning and I *must persevere*.'

So on I ploughed, and on his return from New Zealand Bill continued to come every Tuesday and instruct me. I continued to study the tapes, and Bill tested me from the Manual. I practised my Morse, and as I had passed the Morse exam, I felt more confident of passing the theory exams and therefore put my name forward for the exams due in December.

My Mother wrote to City and Guilds and explained my disabilities. She pointed out that although I was not ready in the previous December, and had been too ambitious and overconfident, could they please send a more sympathetic and experienced examiner than before. The previous examiner was not even a Radio Amateur and had never taken an exam of this nature.

A lady examiner attended. She had a bubbly personality and a keen sense of humour. (She was going to need it!) We got on like a house on fire. I sat the two exams (which were scheduled for one and a half hours each) and completed them both, with a ten-minute break, in two and a half hours.

And I passed!!

I shall always be extremely grateful to this lady, Hilary Clayton-Smith, as Amateur Radio has opened a whole new world to me.

One of the members, Esde Tyler, who writes for the Radio Amateur magazine 'Radcom' wrote a very nice article about me an extract of which is reproduced below, and I became much sought after and popular with other Radio Amateurs.

Severe physical disability from birth proves
no bar to a Class A licence

Gail's Hard Road to Amateur Radio

Bill, G0DVW, (who told us Gail's story) introduced the idea of amateur radio to her and work began. Imagine – an operator who could speak to nearly all foreign stations in their own language! Gail passed the Morse test before taking the RAE, which she passed on the second attempt.

If you hear Gail, she is G0UNF, make her welcome – she has travelled a harder road than most of us – her sense of achievement must be greater. Congratulations Gail. Welcome to the world of amateur radio.

I came to the attention of Alan Bannister, an RA in Manchester, when he heard me talking on the radio to Nathan Penney in Newfoundland and he interrupted our SKED (prearranged, scheduled radio conversation) to ask whether I would like to join a club limited to 20 members, called the Reading (pronounced as the town in Berkshire) Rattle. All the members of this club were also disabled in some way or another. He pointed out that I would be the only female. I, of course, jumped at the chance – 19 males at my mercy! The club sends out monthly news letter cassettes covering a range of subjects, both personal and technical, which are of interest.

From there my involvement with Amateur Radio snowballed, and another club asked if I would like to join. It was the RAIBC (Radio Amateur Invalid and Blind Club). This club is a registered charity (affiliated to the Radio

Society of Great Britain) with no paid helpers. It was formed to help and to provide equipment for disabled radio operators and also to erect aerials for the members who are unable to do so themselves. It does require someone experienced in radio to get them operational. They also run three 'nets' a week. This means that on a certain chosen frequency members can tune in, and an appointed net controller, who is aware of each member's difficulties, inspires confidence and patiently encourages each operator to join in.

It may not sound very important to people who do not know what it involves, but I can assure you it has been a wonderful encouragement to me and has boosted my morale greatly.

The Chairman, Brigadier Johnny Clinch, C.B.E. telephoned one afternoon and spoke with me, kindly offering any assistance required in working my equipment or installation of aerials. He told me that he had lead his brigade on the march past Her Majesty the Queen at Normandy during the D-Day celebrations. I mentioned how lovely she looked in her yellow outfit, and this remark threw him completely.

After finishing our telephone conversation, he immediately phoned Bill Douglas and said, 'Have I got the right person? I thought Gail was blind.'

Bill laughed and said that he had the right person, but that Gail talks as you or I would talk, and she seems no different when you get to know her. 'Her favourite colour is blue.'

So dear Johnny came to see us frequently over the next few months and helped me tremendously. I owe so many friends so much for the help they give so lovingly. No wonder I feel such a special person.

Bill still comes round every Tuesday morning, and we chat together and go on the radio together. My Mother acts as my second operator and tunes the aerials to whatever frequency I am using, and operates the mike for me, as my fingers cannot hold the ON switch when I am transmitting.

Another RA in Guildford, John Edgington, helps me a lot when he has an unusual contact. He phones me and tells my Mother and stands by until I have made contact. I have, therefore, made a great many interesting contacts this way. For example:

An American pilot flying a Hercules Transport plane.

Contacts in Venezuela and Japan.

I have made a friend in Holland – Bob, who is a quadraplegic.

I speak Russian to Lana in Moscow.

There are many others.

John put me in touch with the Vatican City and during our conversation, in Italian, I asked if it would be possible to speak to the Pope. Without hesitation he replied, 'I'm sorry, Gail, but I think he is on a higher frequency to us.' I think he must have been asked this question before.

I also managed to contact a special events station in Atlanta, Georgia, on the last day of the Para Olympics, again with John's assistance.

Every Monday and Thursday morning I look forward to a SKED with my good friend Audrey, and we have a lovely chat. Audrey lives in Poole with her husband Don, who I refer to as her 'handsome prince'. Audrey always has something of interest to tell me as she has five grown-up children and eight grandchildren.

I have also joined the British Young Ladies' Amateur Radio Association and talk to them when I can.

I have another very good friend, Barbara Foote, with whom I exchange audio cassettes. We have the same taste in music.

My powers of conversation were rather stilted but I have found talking on the radio has made an enormous difference to me, especially as no one can take over the conversation from me as I am the only one licensed to talk on the radio. Nathan Penney in Newfoundland has helped me a lot to gain in confidence. I try to contact him most days and we have grown very close. He records music programmes for me every week and posts the tapes, which give me a lot of pleasure. I always close my QSOs (a direct communication) with him by saying 'I just called to say I love you', and he closes with 'Thank you for the pleasure of your company'.

One day a Swedish Radio Amateur broke in and said, 'I wish you would not say that, Gail, you bring tears to my eyes.'

I am extremely grateful to Bill Douglas, who gave me such encouragement and help to pass my exams, and for his continued support.

Whilst we were sitting at the table sending Morse, Bill asked me whether I liked poetry. I said yes, and I like to compose it as well. I could make up a poem for you now if you like. I did so and Bill asked my Mother if she could write it down, which she did and Bill said he would keep it for ever.

The world I live in is a beautiful place,
Where everyone has a lovely face.
The people I meet are loving and kind,
At least, they are so in my mind.

I must have been born under a magical star,
To live as I do and get this far.
So many people have helped on the way,
And you are one, I am happy to say.

So dear Bill, since you asked me to think of a rhyme,
I thought I would do one, in double quick time.
It might not be worthy of Wordsworth or Bacon,
But a lot less time in composing I've taken.

20

We all went off to bed at 11.45 on Saturday 2 March 1996 after a pleasant evening watching three comedy programmes my Mother had videoed previously. I went to sleep immediately, as did my parents, but not before they put on the intercom. Every night, after goodnight kisses all round, my Father calls me on this intercom to make sure it's working.

'Tiger to pussycat. Are you receiving me? Over?'

I reply, 'Pussy to Tiger, I am receiving you loud and clear. Over.'

He says, 'Nighters. Sweet dreams.'

At 1.40 in the morning of 3 March my Father was awakened by a peculiar noise, together with the sound of breaking glass. He nudged my Mother awake and asked if she could hear anything weird. She agreed she could, and jumping out of bed, made their way through the lounge, and sliding back the doors to the terrace went out. To their left they could see flames along the whole roof of the hotel and the windows breaking from the heat. The flames were now only 15 feet away from us.

No fire alarms were sounding.

Before my Mother could get the words out, my Father had come into my room and literally dragged me from my bed into my wheelchair. I was still half asleep. My Mother collected their two dressing gowns and two mohair blankets and they slipped on their shoes, collected Paddy, our 18-year-old cross-breed dog who was deaf and almost blind, and we all made for the front door, with my Father and me leading the way.

The hotel staff were by this time running up and down the corridors and banging on doors shouting, 'Get out, get out, NOW!' The panic had set in and instead of pushing me along the corridor of the flats away from the fire, our instinct was to get down to the ground floor. We dared not use my private lift, so what could we do?

'I shall have to bounce Gail down the stairs in her chair,' said my Father.

Won't someone please tell me what is going on? Bounce me down the stairs? What on earth do they mean? No one is talking to me. What's going on? Where are we going? Please tell me. I was very frightened and they were too busy and shocked to explain.

By this time two of the staff, Jason and Justin, had appeared. 'Can we help you get Gail down the stairs?'

'Please help, but follow my instructions,' said my Father. 'I will go backwards and take the strain, and you hold onto a footrest each in case I fall or the chair goes out of control.'

What a nightmare! I soon found out what they meant by bouncing me down the staircase. Thank goodness we were only on the first floor. By now I was very distressed and traumatised.

The fire brigade appeared with 20 fire tenders and 132 firemen, which was quite a relief. We were all shepherded out of the building onto the car park.

The Fire Officer asked my Father to give them access to our flat, as it was built over the hotel reception area and had a flat roof, and a fire escape down into the main part of the building. So my Father went back to the flat with the firemen and was able to collect some keys belonging to the empty ground-floor flats, away from the fire. We then made our way along the corridor to the flat furthest away from the fire.

Mrs Keeble and Mrs Busby kindly opened their flats for hotel guests and first-floor flat owners. A number of people were in a bad way, shocked and distressed, some crying, some silent, some without shoes and only in their nightclothes. The firemen took over, and they were marvellous. They used our flat to contain the fire, and prevent it spreading. There were hoses everywhere.

My Father left my bedroom light on, as I was very worried about all my tapes and radio equipment, and he said he would keep me informed as to their safety. As long as the light was on, my room was safe. So far so good. Suddenly the Chief Fire Officer appeared with my Mother's handbag. She said to him, 'I could kiss you!'

At four o'clock in the morning I was still in my wheelchair, dropping off to sleep and exhausted. Mrs Keeble offered me her bed – what bliss. I am so grateful to her as she is in her eighties, and had supplied endless cups of tea to everyone. Things had quietened down, and I dropped off to sleep, mentally exhausted. At 4.30 Mrs Wells and others in the flats furthest from the hotel were allowed back to their homes on the first floor. The flat next to ours, which we also own, was intact but badly smoke-damaged, so Mrs Wells opened one of the flats on the ground floor belonging to a friend of hers, and we moved in with Paddy for breakfast.

We were all very tired but relieved no one was hurt or killed. Our flat was a disaster area. Part of the roof was missing, my parents' bedroom destroyed, and the lounge partly destroyed. My equipment was OK.

My Mother said that they should get me out of there as it was affecting me badly. All the talk centred around the

111

fire and the damage to our home. No one could contact us by telephone as the lines were all out, so lots of friends and acquaintances came round to see if they could help.

On the Sunday we went to the Bramley Golf Club for lunch. My Mother said, 'Let's have a bottle of champagne, and work out what we are going to do.'

We decided to move to the Post House Hotel at Guildford, as it is suitable for a wheelchair and they take dogs.

My Mother telephoned on our mobile phone but was told that there was no suitable accommodation before Wednesday of that week. So we had to manage as best we could. My Father and I slept in a smoke-filled bedroom of the next-door flat, and my Mother and Paddy slept in the lounge in an armchair.

Three cheers. On the Wednesday we moved out to the Post House Hotel. That evening we had a celebratory dinner with wine, and went off early to bed in our suite. We had three rooms – two bedrooms, a lounge and two bathrooms. Weren't we lucky?

I shared a king-sized bed with my Mother as I cannot turn over in a strange bed unaided. At three o'clock in the morning I woke up feeling ghastly terrible pains in my stomach.

'Mother,' I said, 'I'm sorry to disturb you, but I do feel sick.'

'Oh, Gail.'

Too late. Sick everywhere.

My Mother washed and changed my nightclothes and I set off again. This time we were prepared. Paddy's water bowl was at the ready. This sickness went on for the rest of the night.

Our kind new doctor had given my parents his home telephone number – little did he realise that we would be taking advantage of it so soon! He came round at 7.30 in the morning. Reluctantly he gave me a painkilling injection, as he knew that if he mentioned going into hospital it would have distressed me further. He told us not to hesitate to call him if I needed him.

I continued to be sick all day, unable to keep even water down, and my Father volunteered to spend the following night with me, as my Mother had had little sleep since the fire. We were awake all night, and the pains got worse. Reluctantly my Father phoned the doctor again at 6.30 in the morning.

He came immediately, and appeared perturbed at my condition. He gave me another injection. My Mother said that she was sorry, but she felt unable to look after me, as it was not fair to me, and that she felt too tired to do her best. I heard the doctor say that he would like to hospitalise me, but was afraid to mention it as it would further distress me.

I called out from the bedroom, 'Doctor, I feel so ill I am quite happy to go to hospital.' The poor doctor was so relieved, and called for an ambulance. Two paramedics arrived, and introduced themselves as Mick and Steve. They chatted away, and took my mind off my discomfort. My Mother came with me in the ambulance, and as we approached Mount Alvernia Hospital she asked why we had turned up a side street.

'We always use the back entrance for admissions,' said Mick.

'Oh, do you indeed?' joked my Mother. 'We are not used to this sort of treatment. Gail wants to make her entrance through the front, with the red-carpet treatment.'

'Sorry,' said Mick, 'but you'll have to go where we tell you to.'

I arrived on the top floor and my Father was horrified. 'Could Gail possibly go on the ground floor? We have just got out of a fire at the Bramley Grange Hotel after

113

bouncing Gail down one flight of stairs, and this is the third floor.'

'I understand your feelings. I will see what I can do,' said the staff nurse.

She returned to say that I could be moved if my Mother and Father could promise some assistance during day and night, which they were happy to do. Apart from the pain, I was quite enjoying myself. All the nurses were very helpful and kind, and with a painkilling drug I was feeling more comfortable, apart from having nothing to eat or drink for three days.

The consultant physician came in to see me, and he was absolutely wonderful. He treated me like a very special person, and talked so nicely to me.

'Well, Gail, I think we had better call in the team on Saturday morning and give you a scan. I have my suspicions, but would like to reserve my opinion until after the scan.'

My Mother stayed with me the first night, for which I was most grateful, and thereafter my parents took turns in sleeping in my room.

I went down for my scan with my Father and they scanned most of my torso. The result was as the consultant had suspected. I had an infected gall bladder and after a few days on a drip, together with antibiotics, I felt a lot better.

The consultant said I came into the category the medical profession called the 'Four Fs' – Female, Fair, Fat and Forty. 'The only thing is, Gail, we will have to dye your hair!' he said jokingly.

I cannot tell you how confident and happy I felt in his care, and all the nursing staff were wonderful to me. Every night they asked me if there was anything I wanted and I replied, 'Yes, I would love a goodnight kiss.' After ten days I was really sorry to leave.

The specialist put me on a fat-free diet for six weeks, and said he would then be ready to operate and remove the gall bladder. So we all returned to the Post House and got on with the job in hand, which was trying to arrange the repairs and restoration to our home. At least there wasn't as much work involved as at Windsor Castle!

One of the planning officers was not very helpful in allowing us to repair the roof to make it habitable, saying that we needed planning permission, and that would take six weeks. Luckily he changed his mind.

Unfortunately, we needed a completely new roof and all the interior required redecorating, together with new ceilings in my parents' bedroom and the lounge. All the furniture and the carpets had been removed, but the flat was the only place I could take a bath, so we came back twice a week.

The time soon passed and I really did not mind the diet. The head chef at the Post House was very considerate and cooked special meals for me. In fact all the staff were wonderful to me, and my friends came to see me, as it did become very boring without my equipment and music, and I was most grateful to them all.

On 2 May I returned to Mount Alvernia, feeling very confident, and met up with all the nursing staff that had looked after me before. They had promised I could return to the same ward – how spoilt can you be!

We followed the same routine as before, my parents sharing the nights. I was only in the hospital for five days, and the surgeon did a wonderful job. I made friends with so many of the staff there, and also with the lady in the room next to me. She had heard me singing to my tapes and asked my parents if she could possibly spend some time with me. We got on like a house on fire, and it certainly made the days fly. I really am very lucky.

We returned to the hotel after another month and moved

back to our flat with everything new or cleaned, and daily routine back to normal.

Just one unfortunate and upsetting event happened – Paddy could not quite make it home again, Bless him. Everyone loved Paddy. He was so loving and well behaved. He just faded away a week before we came home. We all miss him very much.

POSTSCRIPT

Well, this really brings my autobiography up to date, and in a small way I hope that there is someone out there who will draw comfort and inspiration from my story. Always remember that whatever your handicap there is always something you can achieve. As the vicar who took me for my confirmation said, 'I have learnt more from Gail than I have taught her.' What greater compliment can you receive? I really do feel that I have something to offer life.

INDEX